ALICE IN GENDERLAND
Reflections on Language, Power and Control

Published by The National Association for the Teaching of English

First Published 1985
© Authors 1985

ISBN 0 901291 01 3

Illustration: Cath Jackson
Design: John Maddison

Typesetting: Windhorse
Printed in England by David Green Printers Ltd.

Contents

History of the Working Party on Language and Gender

Introduction

A Woman's World   *Julia Hodgeon*   5

Girls don't get holes in their clothes: sex-typing in the primary school   *Hilary Minns*   21

Why doesn't Johnny skip? Or a look at female roles in reading schemes   *Linda Harland*   29

Holding a mirror: a consideration of book provision   *Julia Hodgeon*   35

Literature and sex-bias in the secondary school English curriculum   *Bridget Baines*   45

Stories to grow on   *Elaine Millard*   55

The contribution of books   *Heather Morris*   63

Innocence and experience: the politics of gender and sexual harassment   *Valerie Hey*   71

Tampax and flowers: an approach to pastoral care   *Jan Sargeant*   79

Teacher without a surname   *Margaret Sandra*   85

Structuring stereotyping   *Pat Barrett*   91

Bibliography and further reading   101

The Contributors   106

History of the working party

The Language and Gender working party has been an important voice in the National Association for the Teaching of English over the past five years, and its members have done a considerable abount of work in making contact with a range of teachers throughout the country. The working party was constituted by the NATE Council prior to the York Conference in 1978 and it met officially at that conference, though its roots had been set down at the Durham Conference of 1975, when part of the commission organised by Margaret Sandra and Peter Richards looked at sexist stereotypes and their implications for education.

Implicit in the work of the working party has been the recognition, by past and present members, that sexist language limits the achievements of both sexes, that sexist assumptions in all areas of education circumscribe gender roles, and that the exclusion of women from the printed word denies female expertise and female experience. A commission was organised at the London conference in 1979 entitled "Language and Gender" and at Warwick in 1980, where the working party discussed "Sex Role Socialisation and Knowledge."

Over thirty papers have been written by the working party members and by commission members. Some of these have been published internally and others were included in *Learning to Lose* ed. Dale Spender and Elizabeth Sarah, published by the Women's Press in 1980.

We believe that the series of articles presented here will contribute to the debate and enable readers to learn more about the relationship between language and gender and the meaning it has in their own lives.

Alice in Genderland
Reflections on Language, Power and Control

When the Language and Gender Working Party first considered producing a booklet through which we could share the work we had been doing, we focussed initially on that issue — the connections between language and gender. This was natural enough given the history of the Working Party and our concerns as teachers, researchers, publisher — all of us intimately involved with words. Our original intention was to produce something which explored and exposed the ways in which language has been implicated in the oppression of women and the denial of their history and experience. It would not have been difficult to quote historical examples (the elevation of "he" to include "she" is an interesting case), or give contemporary instances (consider the ways in which terms of abuse are sex-specific). We could then have provided suggestions for monitoring and avoiding these in our speech and writing. This, however, is not what we have produced here.

Our focus changed, partly because a good deal of this ground has now been well-documented in works by Dale Spender and Miller and Swift, but also because in our discussions we discovered we could not isolate language in this way. Language locks into life in a two-way dynamic, both shaping and being shaped. The relationship is complex: sexist language does not create a sexist society, but it is more than just a passive reflection of a reality determined elsewhere. Changing sexist language would not necessarily change the attitudes and assumptions which underlie it, and it is these which must be challenged. What we have attempted here is to describe some of the ways in which the structure and organisation of our educational system, the materials used in it, and the social relations which operate, all combine to produce an environment which prevents many people (both teachers and pupils) from developing their full potential because of their gender. Language is a powerful factor in this, but it is not the only one.

In our writing we have drawn on the many excellent studies already published (see the list of further reading), but above all on our experience as women involved in various aspects of education, as a primary teacher and head, secondary teacher, research student, adviser and educational publisher. Our ideas have been given shape and focus in the extended process of discussions we have shared in the Working Party. One of our main concerns has been to move beyond the stage of describing the problem and to offer positive strategies and ways forward.

The process of sex-stereotyping begins (and continues) far beyond the classroom. Studies have shown that children as young as two will have quite clear ideas on what is and is not gender appropriate behaviour (Serbin, in Marland, 1983). By the time they enter formal school, whether nursery or infant class, these differences are quite marked, as Julia Hodgeon and Hilary Minns demonstrate. What they as teachers can do is not to reverse this process, but, by becoming aware of it, to open it up for possible change.

The ways in which society's sexually differentiated view of "normality" is mediated to children in schools are various. It is done through the hidden curriculum — the hierarchical organisation of schools with men in positions of power, or the different behaviours which are accepted, or even encouraged, from girls and boys. But it is also taught quite overtly in the official curriculum. For English teachers the most obvious aspect of this is the literature which is presented in schools. The gross gender bias and distortions of early reading schemes and many children's books are described here by Linda Harland and Julia Hodgeon. Something not dissimilar goes on every day in secondary schools. Women are under-represented as writers and as characters in fiction, while women's experience is devalued, distorted, marginalised or simply absent. Bridget Baines analyses some popular books used in mixed-sex classrooms and questions the adequacy of their range in providing for the level of stimulus and endorsement of self-image needed by all pupils. Elaine Millard describes the process of encouraging pupils to consider the stereotypes they have learned to adopt, through books which challenge their assumptions. In her lessons she attempts to reveal to the pupils the hidden processes of control, normally in operation and taken for granted as "real" : the stereotyping of male and female. The article from Heather Morris describes some of the current attempts to bring about change in book publishing.

The hidden curriculum of schools affects both teachers and taught. In many ways the experience of female teachers mirrors that of their girl pupils — both are subject to a restricted career choice and prospects, have generally low status and have overtly sexual forms of control directed against them. Schools, as Valerie Hey points out in her article, are not the asexual professional environments they may appear to be. She suggests that the treatment of adolescent females and of female staff is in fact highly sexualised and requires both critical recognition and response, since it contributes directly to female self-doubt and underachievement. Jan Sargeant reflects on the increasingly limited career prospects facing women teachers, while Margaret Sandra describes the hostility and fear her refusal to use either surname or title provoked. It was a direct challenge to the patriarchal status quo which prevails in most educational institutions.

Finally, Pat Barrett describes from her personal position of visiting many educational institutions, the situation of negotiated or unnegotiated power and control in operation and suggests that until the contribution of every person to the educational process is equally valued, children, teachers, caretakers, head teachers, we are locked into non-productive arrangements which prevent growth for all. It is a view well supported elsewhere. The evidence shows "not only that schools treat boys and girls differently, but that they actually make girls and boys more different than the forces of society would otherwise do. Schools act as simplifiers for society's stereotypes." (Marland, 1983)

The use of power and control in the classroom and the wider world, and the link between this power and stereotyping by gender is the central issue. This collection of papers is a contribution to a debate which has been going on for some time and is becoming increasingly urgent.

The articles move from a theoretical, thematic framework into practical assessments of the situations in which we find ourselves. They are all an attempt to move from analysis into practical demonstrations of ways in which change has been attempted. Each one stands in its own right and can be read as an individual voice. This is deliberate and reflects our joint concern to honour each person's contribution to the contexts in which we work.

A Woman's World?
Julia Hodgeon

"Manners are not taught in lessons," said Alice.
"Lessons teach you to do sums, and things of that sort."

Alice in Genderland

Julia Hodgeon is a nursery teacher. On secondment for a year in the County of Cleveland she coordinated a project on sex-differentiation in the early years funded jointly by Cleveland and the E.O.C.

This section forms part of her findings and led to in-service work towards change, with the teachers involved. She observed 364 children in total.

She outlines, here, the sex differentiation which is present and suggests from where change needs to begin.

Nicola: Why is the baby crying?
Jane: She's crying because she wants to go to our Lisa's school. She's fed up of the nursery where the teachers just mind you and you play. Right?

This three year old's perception of the nursery curriculum is one that many adults outside the world of nursery teaching might well share; the very words have the strange ring which comes from the overhearing of adult conversation. Jane probably heard them applied to herself or another child when she appeared to be absorbed in her own affairs. Jane's perception of the curriculum does not chime well with this teacher's.

> "You should give the children as many experiences as possible, and they should freely choose what they want to do. When you think the child is missing out on something, books for instance, you should take it to the child... you should get the child involved... Our function is to extend the children's learning."

This model of the curriculum represented the general view and intended practice of most nursery teachers involved in the research I did on behalf of E.O.C in six nursery units in Cleveland. It seeks to begin from the Piagetian concept of "where the child is" and to build competencies in various aspects, social, linguistic, mathematical, scientific, ethical, aesthetic and physical. The only dispute was about how these competencies might be achieved. In practice, most nursery teachers carried total responsibility for the philosophy and organisation of the nursery. In a real sense it was very much up to them. Head teachers were supportive and appreciative of their work:

> "Teachers have been amazed in the difference in the children who have started school since we had a nursery."

However there was sometimes perceived pressure felt by nursery staffs to prepare children in a more direct sense for school life. This sometimes led to the adaptation of didactic attitudes, to children "settling down", putting play behind them, and beginning to tackle the "real" tasks of schooling to a more content-orientated view of the curriculum. A little time in each session would be given over to sitting together in large groups for story, or copying a sentence, or changing to go to the school hall for P.E. Parents met this strategy with approval, seeing it as the beginning of real schooling. This parent puts the contrast neatly.

> "He didn't want to come this morning because at his other nursery they did writing every day and he says he wants to write. He misses it you see."

The fact was the parent's priority was clear when Andrew refused to have anything to do with drawing/writing activities in spite of active staff encouragement.

Towards a definition of play

> "The trouble with a number of theories of play lies in their tendency to intellectualise the problem." (L.S. Vygotsky: *Thought and Language* 1965)

In one sense Jane was right. In the nursery children play. A number of opportunities are provided and the children are invited, encouraged, expected, to choose a reasonable programme of activity, which through play will lead to learning. The theoretical problem of what play is, the difficulty of finding a way of analysing and tracing a pattern through a play sequence is an ever present one. There seems to be agreement that the element of random practice, of trying out schemas in an apparently aimless way is an important part of learning activity.

> "... play has the effect... of making possible the playful practice of sub-routines of behaviour later to be submitted in more useful problem solving." (J.S. Bruner: *"Play: Its Role in Development and Evolution"*, ed. Bruner, Jolly, Sylva, Penguin 1976)

> ...the essence of play is the domination of means over ends. (Ibid.)

> "early unplayfulness may go with a lack of later originality" (Ibid.)

Much of the work on which these statements are based comes from the observation of animals and of children in experimental situations. The focus of my investigation was the classroom, filled with diverse and sometimes conflicting activities. It was possible to see children establishing themselves in many different ways, often on a deeper level than experimentation.

> *Paul (3.2) 10.20 a.m.*
> With three other boys in wet sand. Much movement pretending to throw sand, giggling. Moves quickly to clay table and back again. Rubs sand onto face and into mouth. Watches nearby adult for reaction. Runs fingers through sand. Pats lightly. Fills bucket, pokes fingers into bucket. Puts sand in mouth again. Watches adult. Scrapes sand around in tray. Shouts to adult. Pretends to throw sand. Puts sand into mouth. Shouts again.
> *10.30 a.m.*

There is more than exploration of materials here. Paul is exploring what power he has, testing it against that of the adult, experimenting with the concept of Paul as a separate human being who can enter into a contest, not sure that it is safe to do so. The sand is his tool.

There was no adult recognition that children were in any way influenced in their choice of tool by their sex or by staff attitudes.

"The boys dress up just the same as the girls... the woodwork, any other activity, there's no difference, none." (Nursery Assistant)

Where differences were noted, it was as if they were taking place in a vacuum, uninfluenced by other children or adults.

"Boys tend to need more physical, active play than the girls, but then the girls tend to go for both anyway... Maybe there's more group work with boys,... girls work more on their own." (Nursery Teacher)

The paradox between the careful matching of curriculum needs through much thought and experience, and the feeling that once this was being attempted the personalities and attitudes of the staff were somehow separate, closed off, was a strange one, but it recurred through many conversations. Staffs constantly undervalued their own roles as powerful models for children and adults.

"What can you do? We only have them for a couple of hours a day."... (Nursery Teacher)

That this time span might have an influence out of all proportion to its length was not much considered.

The women who worked in the six nurseries observed were not untypical of many teachers in primary education. They had a background of certificate training with an arts bias. The nursery assistants were all NNEB qualified (a two-year course).

In order to make a close study of curriculum provision a day was spent in each establishment making a count of how many girls and boys were working with identifiable materials and if adults were working with them. A count was also made of such children as were engaged in washing, toileting, cruising around and pretend. A new count was made every ten minutes.

In many ways this division of provision is artificial and arbitrary; teachers saw much of their work as having wider curriculum application, particularly the linguistic and mathematical aspects.

"Of course language and maths is in everything". (Nursery Teacher)

Conversely some work did not seem to have any tangible expression at all, for example, the social competencies which are essential for school survival. However crude, a way of looking which tries to analyse overt provision is a beginning.

It very quickly became apparent that:—
1. Adults and girls clustered around "quiet" activities e.g. story, drawing and writing, art-related activities.
2. Girls alone often chose domestic-related tasks e.g. pretend based on the homecorner, manipulation with dough or sand.
3. Boys sought independent tasks away from direct adult involvement e.g. large and small construction, energetic outdoor play, woodwork.
4. There was a grey area where there was no strikingly apparent gender differentiation in usage e.g. music, work with food, water.

A group of activities where girls and adults are the most numerous participants

Some aspects of drawing and writing

"Are you going to colour these in now?" (Parent to girl.)

Drawing and writing has a high level of involvement by girls and adults. Provision is varied and careful. Parents encourage their children to take part in an activity with obvious later connections to work in the 3r's. Adults support children by showing obvious pleasure in their achievements.

9.30 a.m. Lyndsey and three other girls sit at the drawing/writing table. An adult joins them. Lyndsey points to her work.

Lyndsey: That's our Michelle.
Adult: What's she doing?
Lyndsey: She's holding a card.
Adult: Did she get lots on her birthday?
Lyndsey: One

Lyndsey draws a series of figures on her paper.

Adult: That's all your family is it? Michelle, Mum, Dad... now we've got them all.
Lyndsey: There.
Adult: That's lovely, we'll put them on the wall.

(Lyndsey is a child with severe social difficulties).

Boys do not work so frequently at drawing/writing, but are welcomed when they do.

Some Aspects of Story

Story is a popular activity with everyone, especially girls. Adults were ready to read story on demand, or ran a constant story session. Girls sometimes appeared to use story as a means of gaining adult attention; though with little real participation.

Julie
9.25 a.m.
Julie has been sitting on the floor with the nursery assistant and Paul for some time. The adult has an arm round each child. She is asking questions, encouraging both children to answer and initiate. Paul does so, working hard. The story ends. Paul leaves.
Adult: Do you want me to read your story now, Julie?

The story begins. Julie now seems more interested, but still behaves passively. She responds to questions by nodding and shaking her head. She refuses eye contact on at least one occasion. Story continues. 9.35 a.m.

Boys when they participate, are active listeners, responding to adult questions, initiating on matters of fact or conjecture.

Peter, Andrew and Christopher
Adult finishes reading *The Very Hungry Caterpillar*.
Peter: Now read that one!
Adult: O.K. We had *The Very Hungry Caterpillar* first didn't we?
(Begins to read *The Best Nest*.
Christopher: Nest the Pest? (laughs).
Text continues, all three children smiling and attentive.
Andrew: That's not a proper house. It's a house where you put letters.
Adult: Confirms and amplifies this. Text continues.
Peter: Birds couldn't do that to my dad! One day he found a bee in our house...
Text continues at conclusion of this long utterance.

By age seven some boys are in significant difficulties with reading. This turning off must occur at the infant stage. There was no evidence that at three and four boys did not handle books for those with little book interest. They did not select themselves as listeners.

Some Aspects of Art-Related Activities.

Go down there and paint your circle. Paint it in. (Student)

Art-related activities form an important part of nursery provision. There is often a wide variety of experimental materials available to the children. At its best and with adult support it provides an extremely flexible series of experiences from which they can learn. At its worst it can be dull and prescriptive with the children acting as incompetent workers to realise an irrelevant adult ideal.

Alice in Genderland

A Face for Father Christmas

John approaches a table where a student is directing children in making Father Christmas's face. The adult picks a margarine carton and draws around it. She writes his name.

Adult: Go down there and paint your circle. Paint it in. (She outlines the circle with pink paint). There you are. Paint in that.
Rachel: (Watching) Just inside there!

An adult is almost always around the art area, since its servicing demands are heavy. There is a high level of participation by girls, particularly in the less messy aspects. Everyone seemed to enjoy clay, fingerpaint, paint mixing from powder and water where much science-based learning was taking place.

Mix your own colour
1.50 p.m. Sarah has been working with powder paint and water since 1 p.m.
Adult: What colour have you made Sarah?
Sarah: Shall I tell you how to mix it? You have red, blue and white like this... I'll show you how to mix yellow. Are you watching?
Adult: What's that Sarah.
Sarah: Let's see. Purple I think.

Sarah continues her work. Meanwhile the adult works with David nearby, diluting paint to an extreme liquid form, floating powder on the surface and helping him to discover that dirty water affects the finished colour. All the children work with enthusiasm.

Socialising is important in art-related activities, both among children and adults.

Painting
Leanne: My sun, look at my sun!
She hands a paintpot to her companion, Tracey.
Adult: Have you got three each now?
Tracey: You have to give me two. There's another one.
Leanne: I'm making a sweetie. Wrap it up. There's my sweetie...

Like drawing and writing and story, art-related activities have adult participation on a high level, thus providing a sheltering environment for those who need it.

Where girls feel confident alone: some aspects of play in the home corner.

Homecorner provision was often elaborate, with child-sized pretend kitchens, bedrooms and dining rooms. Children seemed to adapt the provision freely to suit their own purposes, often incorporating other nursery equipment such as Lego for food.

Girls saw the homecorner as their territory and did not seem to need the sheltering presence of an adult. They often co-operated successfully there. One or two boys would be welcomed into the play, but if a larger group of boys arrived, the girls would leave and continue their play elsewhere. When girls and boys co-operated together the play became prolonged and complex.

Mums and Dads

James: Put the baby in the chair. Am I the daddy?
Michelle: Yes

James picks up the telephone and speaks into it.

James: Yes, the baby is... Yes, I'm coming in a minute. (to Michelle) I'm the dad.
Michelle: Yes of course you are. He's the dad 'an all. (pointing to David).
James: 'Bye I'm going to work. (Goes for a moment. Returns. Stern look, hand on hip).
Michelle: Want a cup of tea?
James: Yes please.

(this play sequence continued for 40 minutes).

The sequence is notable for its length, and the managing attitude of James. Michelle appears conciliatory. Girls seemed to keep to stereotyped roles, cooking, cleaning and caring for babies. No girl went to work, though many of their mothers do. Boys seemed more wide ranging, they cooked and changed babies as well as going to work.

A Group of Activities Where Boys Predominate:—

Some aspects of work with large scale construction

Adult: I think you're going to be a builder, Craig, when you grow up.

Large scale construction includes all the equipment which needs effort to move around and which is designed to be freely adapted for construction purposes e.g. solid blocks, hollow blocks, crates, rostra, stairs, hidey holes. There was a very high level of involvement by boys, girls being only 20 per cent of users. There was no measurable adult involvement.

A clear pattern of usage was evident, which remained constant. Boys would again enter the space reserved for large scale construction and were prepared to defend it against all female intrusion.

Alice in Genderland

In the Playground
Two boys are outdoors on wooden boxes. Teacher joins the children on the boxes.
David: Only boys can go there.
Teacher: Well I've got trousers.
David: (thinking carefully): Well it's only for people with shoes like mine and Paul's!

Boys would then handle the materials, constructing a boat, a car, a ship or a house. In its finished form, this would be the basis for further play. Later adults and girls would be allowed to participate without challenge as the boys' interest waned. Boys would withdraw, leaving girls in possession of a base for verbal/imaginative play or as in this example, somewhere to sit for story.

Boating
James and Andrew work in the block area. They make a flat floor with complex additions.
James: A bridge, we need a bridge.
He tries to bridge the space between the construction and the door.
James: It (block) will go through the letter box and the teacher will fall over. That's what. Look, I'll just go and get Mrs. B.
James: Mrs. B., are you coming in the ship boat, the pirate boat?
Mrs. B. joins the boys, bringing two girls with her.
Natalie: There's the books, up there. The shark can't get them.
Mrs. B. reads a story. All the children listen. It ends.
Andrew: Do you know I need that whale there?
Mrs. B.: Is this the boat? It's a bit squashed.
James: It's full, too full. Nobody else can come on. You'll have to go. I need to get out.

Girls were rarely seen to be having the handling experiences crucial to learning with this kind of material, simply adapting what was already there to their own purposes. Sometimes the original builders would return and demand their own boat or whatever back. There is an example on videotape of a boy alone successfully removing three girls in this way.

Some aspects of work with small-scale construction
There is usually lavish and varied provision of this kind. It includes Lego, plastic Meccano and Mobilo plus a variety of less well-known equipment. Some systems like Meccano use tools; others like Constructor rely on the element themselves to fit together in a number of ways. Children find them very adaptable

for use as food or weapons, or to carry around in the hand or pocket. Over 60 per cent of users of small scale construction were boys; there was some adult involvement, and girls used these materials much more freely than large scale construction. Girls appreciate Lego particularly, using it with adult support as problem solving material.

A House in the Jungle
Adult: Susie, do you need another door?
Susie: There's two houses there. I want one of them coaches.
Adult: One of these? Shall I fix it on?
Susie: Now people. How can they get up? There's no ladders?
Adult: Is that going to work?
Susie: We'd better fix it next to the door...

Often their work is complex and concentrated:—

People on a Bus
Nicola has worked in the Lego for 35 minutes. She searches in the tray of Lego. Chooses four bricks. (Talks to self).
This is a bus.
(Makes person taller with brick).
You drive.
Guess how big it is now.
(Piles bricks to make one figure very tall).
Look how big it is now. I've put another one on. Can you see, one's bigger than the other one.

Perhaps girls are attracted to Lego because it is ordered and quiet, often set out on a table, and with some adult support.

It was sometimes possible to see raw materials used for different purposes by boys and girls. In the following example the boy seems to be using a patterning schema, the girl is experimenting with social and imaginative thinking.

A boy and girl play in parallel with coloured wooden rods
Mark, kneeling on the floor, makes a line with 2 long rods.
Debbie spoons short rods up into a pan.
Debbie: We're going to make the dinner.
Mark makes △ — a three sided figure.
Debbie: There's some dinner.
She goes off with the pan.
Mark makes a long line of rods punctuated by cubes.

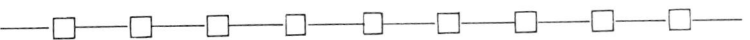

He kneels and looks at the rods. Collects up cubes and holds in cupped hand. Drops one cube. Experiments, poking it with index finger into the carpet. Alters line arrangements slightly. Debbie comes back. Mark scrapes the rods together. Both go to drinks table.

Some Aspects of Working With Wood

"I don't know that it's safe." (Parent)

Benches, tools, and scrap wood for children to experiment with were provided in two nurseries. There was some adult anxiety about the safety of children using tools; staff worked to encourage them to work safely and to co-operate on a mature level. Adult involvement was therefore supervisory. Boys clearly felt confident, and were ready to take over from girls if they showed any sign of diffidence. Girls did not see themselves as woodworkers, even *with* the support of an adult.

Michael and Helen work at the bench

Adult: Show me how you can hammer, Helen. Is it tight in the vice, Michael?
Michael: My piece of wood is the right way round.
Helen: Can I have the saw?
Michael: You need it (vice) wide, why don't you cut it there?

Helen saws.

Helen: I can't get the wood cut. I can't do it.
Adult: Have you tried to? Sometimes it takes ages.
Michael: Here you are (takes saw).
Helen: Look he's done it for me.
Michael: Do you want me to do this for you?
Helen: Yes, cos I can't saw can I?
Michael: I told you, put it in the vice or it will move. I'll put it in the vice...

The children had no female model of a woodworker, since the adults did not really participate. This perhaps leads to lack of development, since most woodwork consists of hammering and attempts at sawing.

Some Aspects of Outdoor Play.

"I'm the King of the Castle!" (Tony.)

Gender stereotypes were clearly displayed when children worked outdoors. Provision was generous in terms of space and equipment with an important aim the development of large muscle movement. An adult would normally supervise the outdoor play space and in good weather the children would be free to choose indoor or outdoor activity.

Boys would, at the signal for play outdoors, rush and seize upon the most valued pieces of equipment, not hesitating to take them from girls or smaller boys. They would shout and rush around. Girls tended to stay near the adult, talking or playing with her.

A chilly windy day.
Boys play football, rough and tumble in the sand pit, ride bikes, shout and run around. Girls swing, push prams, play a game of bowling hoops with an adult. No play across sexes.

The supervising adult has difficulties should she wish to actively involve herself in outdoor play. Supervision for the sake of *safety* is important when children are climbing, jumping, running. Involvement in play may cut down the supervisory element to dangerous levels.

Sometimes adults showed unnecessary solicitude at venturous play by girls.

Climbing and balancing.
Adult: Nicola, careful, are you O.K?
Rolling in the barrel
Adult: Ruth, do you want to come out? Are you alright?
Boys were not asked these questions.

A grey area; curriculum aspects where gender bias was not so obvious

These were: work with food; making sounds; sand play; water play; scale version toys; structured materials.

Adult intervention was of various kinds:—

1 Initiating and leading
   Adult: Grate your cheese like this, Robert. That's it. It breaks into little pieces, so it will cook better.
   Robert: Mine's done. What will you cook for the children this afternoon?
   Adult: Cheese omelettes again I think. Can you fetch the little plastic cartons, the first omelette's nearly done.
   Robert: Do you mean these...?

2 Supervising without handling materials often leading to verbal/imaginative play sequences
   The diver and the shark
   Three boys are at the water tray with an adult.
   Adult: Is the diver going? He's gone. Rescue him. Get the lifeboat out. Is he O.K.? We nearly lost him.
   Tom: He's a shark and he's killed him at the bottom of the sea. He's had it.
   Adult: Oh I don't know; if he's got his diving suit on...

3 Supporting children so that a task can be completed.
   Jigsaws
   Andrew empties his completed puzzle from the tray.
   Adult: Are you trying to do it quicker every time?
   John: I've done mine! It's missing, that.
   Adult: Put it up the right way, then you'll know what's missing.
   John: I'll go and look in the drawer.
   Adult: O.K., and tell me if the piece is there...

In all these interventions the adults displayed the sex bias demonstrated in other curriculum areas; they constantly swung children towards verbal/imaginative outcomes, neglecting possible openings for science-based learning; they spent little time handling materials alongside children thus failing to present girls with a model of a problem-solving learner with wide interests.

Wandering, Cruising, Toileting

There is less wandering around and general non-participation by children than teachers assume. Many children who appear to be purposeless are searching: for an adult, for a particular friend, for a new activity. Children will articulate these purposes if asked. There seems to be no sex difference. The adult "just checking" will see an apparent difference however: — girls will appear to be busy or, if not, unobtrusive or diffident. They will not be a source of annoyance to others. Boys who are now participating might well be indulging in "unsocial" behaviour as far as a classroom is concerned: chasing, noise or playfighting.

All children considered to be wandering or engaged in what teachers consider unsocial behaviour will be actively encouraged to join in other activities. Parents have a phrase for a well-occupied, co-operative child; "Play nice", they say as they go.

Children are encouraged to be independent in toileting and washing from their earliest nursery days. Girls in particular are urged to "get on with it". Boys may be helped with zips, braces and tight waistband buttons.

The Curriculum: Some Gender Implications

Although one should not attempt to make too simple a connection between girls' marked lack of participation in science-related activities at this age and their patchy achievements in these fields in their later education, it is clear that there is a ready acceptance on their part of girls' and boys' territory in the nursery classroom.

> Girls' (and their teachers') territory is that of domestic/caring/sharing/imaginative activities. Boys' territory is that of constructive/experimental/practical/problem-solving activities.

Children use the overt provision for many purposes, sometimes not clear to an observer, so the compartments are not water-tight. There remains male willingness to defend the block area against all female incursion, a feature of every establishment visited, and the constant adult turning aside of children's schemes into the verbal/imaginative model.

Girls seemed to need the closeness of the adult and sought to work near her. They thus spent most of their time in the activities which interested the *adult* or at least observed them at close quarters. Products of their own stereotyping, adults devoted themselves to activites which might have been predicted, story, drawing and writing, music. Often the adult *was* taking part here, and was not merely supervising or talking. When she took part in large construction, woodwork, sand or water, it was often with the expressed intention of developing the children's *language* and there was little handling of materials on her part. If girls are using the adult as a model (and this did seem to be the case, very much so), then they have a picture of a caring, skilled handler of social relationships who is good at reading, writing and drawing, but does not seem confident in some other major aspects of human knowledge and applications.

Does the equation:
> Boys can do most things: girls can do some things well but not others

begin to operate at age three and four?

Girls Don't Get Holes in their Clothes

Sex-typing in the primary school

Hilary Minns

"Then you'd better not fight today", said Alice, thinking it a good opportunity to make peace.
"We *must* have a bit of a fight, but I don't care about going on long," said Tweedledum. "What's the time now?"
Tweedledee looked at his watch, and said "Half-past four".
"Let's fight till six, and then have dinner", said Tweedledum.
"Very well," the other said, rather sadly, "and *she* can watch us..."

Alice in Genderland

I wrote this piece when I was teaching a class of 7-9 year olds. In it I have tried to describe some of the ways the children and I worked together as we became increasingly aware of what it meant to grow up male or female. Working with these young children through successes and failures, and later writing about them, showed me how diffifult it was for them to grow up free, in the face of relentless pressure to conform, to take on their "appropriate" gender role. At eight years of age many had stereotyped themselves.

But young children can be helped towards an understanding of society's expectations of them, and what follows describes some of the writing and discussion that took place in our classroom over one term.

Girls Don't Get Holes in Their Clothes

"There's somebody's writing here with no name on," said Owen. "It must be one of the girls, anyway."
"Why?"
"Cos it's neat."

He was probably right, too. That's the sad part of it. Louise explains it like this:

> I think boys are messier than girls because they get holes in their jumpers and trousers and their shirts and girls never get holes in their clothes and boys are messier than girls because boys push other boys over but girls play nicely but boys dont but boys think they are ace because they think that they can do everythink but they cant because they cant do a headstand or a bridge so they can not do everythink.

Aged between seven and nine the children I teach, depending on their sex, dress differently, play differently, and with different toys, are more or less strictly supervised at home, are used as baby-sitters or not, and have learned what it is to be masculine and feminine. Dawn and Samantha wrote about what they think a tomboy is:

> A tomboy is someone who has a brother. My friend's a tomboy but I don't think she is because she has not got a brother, so she is not a tomboy.
>
> You have to have a brother before you can be a tomboy because you will know what to do. I've got two brothers and I go with them when they play out and I play football and I climb trees. I go butterfly catching. I do lots of things like boys.

The children's sex-role behaviour is well established before they come to school.

Julia:	Miss it was very sad when Charlotte died. I... everyone, nearly everyone cried.
Clayton:	Only the boys didn't cry 'cos they were brill.
Boys:	Yeah.
David:	True Clayton.
Clayton:	We don't cry like girls. They're babies.
Boys:	True.
Samantha:	Miss I think it's a lump-in-your-throat story 'cos when you're halfway through you have to go (swallow) — like that.
Karen:	Miss I think erm why the boys didn't cry is because the girls are more sensitive than boys at stories like that.

Alice in Genderland

Tracey: I think I know why girls sometimes cry cos they take things more serious than boys do.
Julia: They don't have feelings.
Tracey: They take it more seriously like when erm Cathy Cathy died in er *Wuthering Heights* I started to cry a bit cos I like Cathy. She was mischievous like me.
H.M.: The story was written by E.B. White. Samantha and Natasha and David said "she" when we talked about the author and Clayton said he thought it was probably a man.
Clayton: Cos it's more like a man's story. Men don't cry when... spiders die. Women do, they're so stupid.
Samantha: Miss it's like when you go to the wedding. I didn't know whether to cry or laugh. It's like that in some stories as well.
Clayton: It's not a lady's story. It's not a lady's story.
H.M.: What's a lady's story Clayton.
Clayton: Well you wouldn't get a woman writing about a pig would you?
Karen: Miss and I know why that is
Nathan: They smell
Karen: Cos ladies don't like pigs as much as men, cos boys are pigs.

Girls, then, are sensitive, clean, thoughtful; boys are swaggering, tough and dominating. Perhaps it is particularly hard for the boys in my class to see themselves differently. Janet Robyns has written that "no one has made it right for (boys) to try and find valuable those characteristics our society have labelled as female." They certainly aren't allowed expressive behaviour. Even a book about birds from our junior reference libaray shows them how they must be when they grow up:

> The cockerel, the father of the chicks, is the head of the family. Just look at him, with his tall red comb, the long claws, the beautiful feathered tail, his size! He looks so full of importance.

The mother hen, in contrast, is "anxious and nervous about her little ones". (*The Little Chick*)

A large number of our story books at school, including those of high literary merit which are beautifully illustrated, still present children and adults in stereotyped activities, rigidly divided into masculine and feminine worlds, and often at the expense of the female:

> Once upon a time there was a farmer called Jan, and he lived

all alone by himself in a little farmhouse.

By and by he thought that he would like to have a wife to keep it all shiny and pretty.

So he went a-courting a fine maid, and he said to her: "Will you marry me?"

"That I will, to be sure", she said. (*Hereafterthis*)

Domesticity and what Alleen Pace Nilsen calls the "cult of the apron" is widespread. The mother in *Can I Keep Him?* is seen sweeping, cleaning the lavatory, tidying the cupboards, vacuuming, washing up and scrubbing on her knees. Her relationship with her son is shown to be that of servant to master. The perceptive *No Kiss for Mother* examines this relationship more closely. It's a book about cats and it's about other things too.

> But Piper's mother, Mrs. Velvet Paw, needs no alarm clock. She gets up every day at the same time, except on Sunday mornings when they all brunch in bed... Mother Paw has neatly laid out his clothing, cleaned and pressed the night before... and every morning, with renewed rage, he crumples and rumples his clothes behind his mother's back... "you just enjoy hurting my feelings", Mother Paw says between sniffles.

An edition of the *Encyclopaedia Britannica*, published in 1800, has this to say about the sex roles:

> The man, more robust, is fitted for severe labour, and for field exercise: the woman, more delicate is fitted for sedentary occupations, particularly for nursing children. The man, bold and vigorous, is qualified for being a protector; the woman, delicate and timid, requires protection. Hence it is that a man never admires a woman for possessing bodily strength or personal courage; and women always despise men who are totally destitute of these qualities. The man, as a protector, is directed by nature to govern; the woman, conscious of inferiority, is disposed to obey. Their intellectual powers correspond to the destination of nature. Men have penetration and solid judgement to fit them for governing, women have sufficient understanding to make a decent figure under a good government; a greater portion would excite a dangerous rivalry between the sexes, which nature has avoided by giving them different talents.

Unfortunately these nineteenth century attitudes are still prevalent in much literature that is written for young children. Marriage is still the main female occupation open to girls, according to these books. They may also become mothers, grandmothers, shop assistants, teachers or nurses. None of these occupations is given importance, because they are often done by women; this message is carried implicitly through many of our books. A large number of our reference books are similarly male-defined, both in content and in their use of language and illustrations. A series of books describing occupations will often include such jobs as: the farmer, the lorry driver, the coal miner, the fireman, the shoemaker, the garage mechanic, the astronaut, the fitter, the builder's labourer, the dustman, the airline pilot, the train driver, the postman, the policeman, the fisherman, the nurse.

Titles often cover exclusively male occupations or occupations where female workers are not acknowledged to exist — there are plenty of postwomen around. Frequently, no mention is made of females doing work, either in text or illustration. These books convey the implicit message to children that males are more important than females and have open to them a whole range of interesting jobs that are closed to women. Where females are portrayed they are commonly seen as housewives and mothers, carrying out low level domestic tasks. There is little presumption that they are highly likely to be in paid employment or that the job of child-rearing is itself a responsible one which is intellectually and emotionally demanding. One book on our shelves, *Famous Writers*, published by MacDonald Educational, is especially interesting. Although the editorial board was made up of two women and one man, and in spite of the fact that the editor-in-chief was a woman, *all thirty-four writers in the series are male*. The introduction to the book reads as follows:

> Man is a born story-teller. It is not enough for him to do things, he must also tell stories about the things he has done...

In this book then, women are doubly excluded; their contribution to writing is unrecognised and the use of the word "man" as representative of human beings, and of "he" as a neutral pronoun, have the effect of excluding females from any concern with story-telling and writing.

All around them at school the children see a system of hierarchies operating, and some of these are based on sex. Our head is male, our caretaker is male — at our school he and his wife seem to share responsibility for the running of the school, yet he is the caretaker and she is the caretaker's wife, and the children know this. All the low-status jobs in our school belong to females; cooks, dinner ladies, cleaners. The caretaker's daughter willingly helps to clean the school; the son plays football, equally willingly, on the school fields.

When I first became aware of what was going on, and how ideas were being constantly reinforced by the kind of society within school, I tried to *make* the girls and boys in my class behave differently, by doing things together. I tried to make them line up for assembly in mixed-sex lines, even though they rebelled. I tried to make them get changed in mix-sex groups, and they hated that even more. I gave up after a while when I realised that none of this was helping them to change from the inside and it wasn't showing them new ways of how boys and girls can live together. All it was doing was making them feel threatened and embarrassed. So I don't do those sorts of things any more: I'm more likely now to help them towards an awareness of the similarities between the sexes, rather than the differences, by encouraging them to work together in mixed-sex groups: so they're not just meeting head-on for the sake of it, but learning that they can work together at a common interest. I try to be alert to possible ways of helping them to come to terms with sexism *in their own way*, and in terms that they understand. For example, Sharon, who is seven, found a picture in the Sun newspaper of a bare-breasted woman. She showed it to me:

Girls Don't Get Holes in Their Clothes

"I was putting this newspaper on the painting table and they laughed at it," she complained.
"Why has it upset you?" I asked her.
"Because they're making fun of her," she said.
"What do you want to do about it?" I asked.
"I'm not sure," she said, "but I'll keep it in my tray till tomorrow and think about it."

The following day she wrote a letter to the *Sun*:

Dear Sir or Mrs,
    Would you stop putting these DISGUSTING pictures in the newspapers, because it is making fun of women and girls *please*.

Within days five children, three girls and two boys, had opened a *Complaints about Sexism* file and two more children wrote letters to the *Sun*. Here's one of them:

Sir or Mrs,
    Why do you put women in the Sun because you like it well if you do like it stop it because I do not like it and if a woman writes a letter to ask if they can have their photograph taken you should write a letter back and say no and just why why why do you put women in the Sun just stop it because I said so.

The children received replies to their letters. This is one of them:

There is nothing "rude" about our pictures of unclothed ladies and on occasion men as the Daily Male feature. The model girls who pose for the pictures are not being made fun

Alice in Genderland

of at all. They are greatly respected for their beauty and every year we get hundreds of letters from girls whose ambition is to have their picture on Page 3 of the *Sun*.

If we stopped putting these pictures in the paper many of our readers would write and complain — and not all would be from male readers.

The children then wrote to the Press Council and did their own survey of male and female heroes in story books they read. This was the result:

> We have done a survey on 100 books to find out about how many female heroes there were in different books and this is what we found:
> 62 male heroes   26 female heroes   12 of both
> There were more males than females.

It's taken us two terms to get this far and all the time I'm conscious that the influences outside my classroom are very much stronger than mine; but that won't stop me from challenging the categories and perceptions the children meet outside, and if they begin to probe and question for themselves, as Sara does in the piece that follows, then it's perhaps not a bad beginning.

> My brother won't let me marry my Sindy doll to his action man. I feel left out because I promised Sindy that she could marry him. Why won't he let me? Why shouldn't I? What made him stop me? Why shouldn't a girl play with an action man? I think that us children should have toys to share. My brother won't let me play with any of his toys because I am a girl.

Why doesn't Johnny skip?
Or a look at female roles in reading schemes.
Linda Harland

"Of course you know your A B C?" said the Red Queen.
"To be sure I do," said Alice.
"So do I," the White Queen whispered: "we'll often say it over together, dear. And I'll tell you a secret — I can read words of one letter! Isn't *that* grand?"

Alice in Genderland

In this paper Linda Harland shows how sexist influences in the educational system parallel and perpetuate the values of wider society, in particular the traditional stereotyped male/female roles.

She undertakes a critical analysis of the textual and pictorial messages of reading schemes, bringing out the emphasis placed on false "differences" between boys' and girls' behaviour, ambitions and interests.

The analysis underlines the obvious dangers of presenting children with this material and shows how little resemblance the "worlds" of these books bear to reality. The perpetuation through these books of a white, middle-class society with its rigidly defined sex roles can be extremely damaging when it is offered as the norm for all children in their first stages of reading.

In infant and junior schools the main instrument for helping children to become literate is the commercially produced reading scheme. Although schools are beginning to reappraise the efficacy of such schemes, current financial constraints mean that few have been entirely discarded. Many children in their early school years will have access to these books only. Apart from the minority who have a wide choice available at home, the adventures of Billy Blue Hat, Ben and Lad, Gregory the Green, and stories read by the teacher constitute the world of books for most children in their early years at school.

If we accept this we must ask what view of the world may be gleaned through such books, and whether we can do anything in schools to prevent children from acquiring the distorted outlook presented in reading schemes. It will be useful to examine some of these reading schemes, and the rationale behind them, to see if we can detect evidence of sex-role stereotyping. We will then look at the effect which literature can have on children's views of themselves in the world, and what we as teachers can do about it.

The Educational Publishers Council (1981) discusses the definition of stereotyping with reference to children's books. They present stereotyping as a "standardised view based on received assumptions which are automatically applied to all circumstances and take no notice of individual differences. They are clichés." Sex-role stereotyping, therefore, categorises male and female characteristics and roles, either by misrepresentation, or, more commonly in children's books, by omission.

During the 1970s there was considerable research into sex-stereotyping in books for children, both in Britain and the United States. Most of the earliest criticisms were based on the *Ladybird Key Words* reading scheme. Cannan (1972) felt that the stories in this scheme presented "precisely the difference between boys' and girls' roles and mothers' and fathers' roles." For example:—

> "Peter has to help Daddy with the car, Jane has to help Mummy in the house."
> "'Yes,' said Peter, 'You make the tea and I will draw."
> "Yes. I will be like Mummy and get the tea," says Jane."

It is very easy to find such scenes throughout the scheme, and the publishers have recently brought out a new version which they claim is more in line with present day reality. Ladybird was not alone in containing many extreme examples of sex-role stereotyping. *Janet and John, Happy Venture, Ready to Read, Breakthrough to Literacy, Nippers,* as well as *Ladybird,* were analysed by Glenys Lobban (1974) in terms of girl/boy, male/female adult roles. She found that in all schemes male-female activities were rigidly differentiated and did not show the world as it was. When she considered two more recent schemes in 1976 — *Language in Action* and *Pirates* — the ratio of male to female characters was 5:1.

These studies were carried out a decade ago and we might reasonably assume that publishers would have become sensitized to criticism and to a change in the perceptions of women's roles. Unfortunately the scheme which is becoming to the 1980s what Ladybird was to the early 1970s — *Ginn 360* — appears to present sex-roles in no more enlightened terms than its predecessors. This ubiquitous, all-enveloping scheme, which has been marketed aggressively, reveals a very disappointing range of female roles.

Male/female roles analysed in Ginn 360
Levels 1-9

Men's/boys' roles	*Women's/girls' roles*
playing football	Washing clothes
driving a car	housework
cleaning a car	preparing food
out at work	skipping
piloting helicopters	teaching
rescuing	in wheelchair
playing with train set	
gardening	
working with animals	
policeman	
demolition crane driver	
building site workers	
playing with space ship	
making signs	
forester	
postman	
inventors	
airport workers	
bulldozer driver	

If we examine one of these books more closely we can see the extent to which females are omitted. "Across the seas", Level 9, Book 5, one of Ginn's occasional acknowledgements of other cultures, contains four stories. The first story is about an Indian boy, Ram, a wise and talented older brother, with a younger sister, Deepti, whose only role in this tale is to think "he was the best artist in all India." Story two is about a boy and girl living on the coast of France. The girl is rescued from the perils of the sea by the boy's astuteness. In the third story no women appear at all, and in the fourth story, featuring a boy and his relationship with a male animal, human and animal mothers are mentioned incidentally.

Ginn 360 is not the only scheme to see women and girls only as admirers, comforters and providers of food for males. *One, Two, Three and Away* by Sheila McCullagh, a very popular scheme in infants and lower juniors, seems to have the same kind of myopia regarding the female role. In the teachers' handbook to this series the setting is presented as being a "half-fairy tale" so that "stories about the adults and children can reflect the experiences of children from many different backgrounds." (McCullagh, 1975). If this is so one can only wonder at the paucity of experience that exists for girls to relate to. The main characters are three boys — Billy Blue Hat, Roger Red Hat, Johnny Yellow Hat and one girl, Johnny's sister Jennifer. They are surrounded by parents, grandparents and characters in the village, most of whom are male. The structure of the scheme is made quite intricate by the addition of supplementary material, which is still being published. The concession to a multi-ethnic approach is made by the addition of three new characters, Ramu, Sita and Gopal — two boys and a girl.

If we look at the twelve books which constitute the core of the scheme we find that in four of these books no women appear at all; in six of these books women appear either as mothers providing tea or scolding the boys after their adventures, or as onlookers. Jennifer is to be seen occasionally holding her skipping rope, hovering on the edge, and staying out of any trouble. The only book in which she takes a leading role is one where she looks, listens, and follows a cat through the wood at night, while wearing a nightdress — hardly the kit for action.

It is clear from the above examples that fifty-one per cent of the population is drastically under-represented in books which are read by a large proportion of children in schools, and which are still being purchased in great numbers. We may ask whether this matters, or whether this sex-stereotyping and omission has any influence on children's attitudes. Several studies have been carried out on the effect of sexist and non-sexist stories. Rosemary Stones (1983) summarises this research which proves very clearly that children's books have an important part to play in the way children view themselves in the male or female role. It was also revealed that non-sexist books could have a positive effect in enabling boys and girls to become more confident so that they could carry out a wider variety of roles.

It is important to realise that the rigidity of sex-role stereotyping is not only harmful to girls. Boys may feel equally inhibited by the pressure to appear brave, fearless and smart if they see no other role model in books. Eleanor Maccoby (1966) put it most strongly when she said that rigid sex-role definitions not only foster unhappiness in children but also hamper the child's fullest intellectual and social development.

Alice in Genderland

If we accept that reading schemes show a great deal of rigid sex-stereotyping and that this is likely to adversely affect children's development we must then ask what is to be done, given the large number of scheme books in schools. The first suggestion must be to consider very carefully whether the future purchase of such schemes can be justified. There are so many good, "real" books being published that it is hard to understand how schemes — severely limited in language and, as we have seen, attitudes — find their way into schools. If schools cannot afford to discard their schemes we should try to supplement them with as many non-stereotyped books as possible, and to discuss the limitation of role representation with the children. Even very young children are suprisingly astute when made aware of what weaknesses to look for. Perhaps children can rewrite some of the stories, substituting girls for boys, women for men. Does this make any difference? Why did the author not do this in the first place? We cannot start heightening children's critical faculties at too young an age. Where better to start than with a critique of a reading scheme? If Johnny was reduced to skipping and watching, there is a chance that he might quickly look for an alternative style of literature.

Holding a Mirror
A Consideration of Book Provision
Julia Hodgeon

There was a book lying near Alice... and she turned over the leaves, to find some part she could read, "— for it's all in some language I don't know," she said to herself.

Alice in Genderland

This chapter is a further extract from the work of Julia Hodgeon in her project on sex differentiation in the early years. She examines the books in use in the six nurseries she studied and suggests ways in which they might be evaluated and dealt with by adults and children.

Mrs. Mudd had to work very hard looking after them all. S.
(Lavalle: *Everybody Said No,* Black)

One of the peepshows that children have onto the world outside their own experience is the picture that comes from the books that adults share with them. The selection of books for nursery use may be a chancy affair. Responsibility for choice may rest with the head teacher or with the teacher responsible for language in the infants school; sometimes the nursery teacher is free to choose or at least to make requests. My observations in six Cleveland nursery units showed that divergence was wide between the best provision, an up-to-date stock of picture books as numerous as that in many infant schools, and the poorest, which was founded upon the *Mr. Men* series with perhaps a dozen library books as supplement.

Given that the literature on the general topic of sex stereotyping in books for young children is plentiful, it was decided to look carefully at the actual book provision with the aim of identifying a set of criteria as a guide for future book selection. Some limit had to be imposed on the survey: it was decided that the examination should be confined to the fifty most popular books in the nursery with the best provision. These were the books that the children chose most often to be read aloud to them or to read themselves to an adult. This selection provided a wide range of materials in everyday use by children.

Examination of the text considered the following points:

What was the balance of female and male characters?
What were the male characters? What were they doing?
What were the female characters? What were they doing?
What might children be expected to learn from the above?

The balance of female and male characters

There was, over the fifty books, a heavy predominance of male characters, 126 as against 71 females. Other characters had no sex specified: a Wild Thing is a Wild Thing, only the group identity being significant.

In eleven of the books there were no female characters at all, in one there were no males. Overall males seem over-represented, a possible indication of their relative importance.

Who are the male characters and what are they doing?

The fifty picture books presented a wide range of male characters, from boys and men to mice, cats and bears. Often animals are used in stories for very young children to distance the action and to make safe what might be threatening. So Harry, in *Harry, The Dirty Dog* is a dog rather than a child in a story about running away from home and returning to be forgiven. Certain animals seem to fit certain images: dogs are almost always male and have an active life-by-the-throat projection, like Harry or Spot in *Where's Spot*. Bears, again popular characters, are male, not very bright, and cuddly: see *The Bear's Toothache* and *The Winter Bear*. Sometimes it is more difficult to know why animals were used rather than people, but there is also the opportunity for expressive delight as with the birds in *Are You My Mother?*.

Male animals share the characteristic of the boys and men in other books and have no identifiable animal traits at all. Young males are active creatures seeking out the vicissitudes of life and learning from them.

Realistic and fantastic characters share these attitudes. Mickey goes to find out what is in *The Night Kitchen*, he doesn't hide his head under the covers. Bernard, in *Not Now Bernard*, establishes his identity through aggression, until this wears itself out. *I Wish I Had Duck Feet* is a power fantasy about getting the better of the local bully. Consistently cheerful, these "lads" are never more than slightly discomfited and not for long: they're soon smiling again. Though not always very bright (see the male cat in the *Meg and Mog* stories who can't hold on during a broomstick ride), they can be resourceful when necessary. The boy in *The Plant Sitter* goes to the library to seek information about pruning and propagation; the mice in *Atkil's Bicycle Ride* improvise parachutes from plastic bags. Fond of play with cars, aeroplanes, bikes and balls, they do not like flowers, *No Roses for Harry*. James, who loses his model aeroplane in *James and the Model Aeroplane* and cries, is highly unusual.

Men are almost always fathers, though the selection also includes a conventionally awful pirate and various other seafarers, a king, a rat-catcher and a nursery teacher. Fathers step in when women and children can't cope. Sometimes "fierce-looking", men befriend weaker and helpless souls, sometimes females. They rescue lost aeroplanes and sort out problems when everything goes wrong, while the women look on: *When Willy Went To The Wedding*. They make important decisions about what children should learn: the father in *Topsy and Tim's Monday Book* teaches his boy a lesson by letting him have his own way. They teach the important lessons of life: father cat does this for the silly kitten in *The Kitten Who Couldn't Get Down*. Sometimes they kindly undertake household tasks: King Rollo and his magician wash up for the female cook as a "special treat".

Adult males work, but invisibly, going off smartly dressed and not being around for much of the time: see *The Plant Sitter*. This mysterious work earns them the privilege of sitting around the house reading the papers, watching television or writing to their bank managers (*Everybody Said No, The Plant Sitter, Not Now Bernard*). They often look bad-tempered at being interrupted or disturbed in these activities. They like to arrange things (*Fourteen Rats and a Ratcatcher*), they like fishing (*I Bet I Could*) and otherwise like to be left in peace.

There is an intensifying mismatch with the reality of many of our children's home lives, where there is a regular male presence. Many fathers are out of work and are at home a good deal. They are learning, if only to keep themselves sane, to take on a much more active household role.

Who are the female characters and what are they doing?

The range of female characters is much narrower than that of the males. Predominantly they are mothers and female children. There are also witches, teachers, a few animals — almost always cats, relatives, one old lady, one fairy and one cook.

Witches are an interesting group, for which there is no equivalent male group. The one wizard (in *Atkil's Bicycle Ride*) is kind, gentle and caring. Witches are old and ugly. Teachers are universally condescending and awful. Which of these professional women would you rather be?

Young female characters are a fairly colourless lot, who stick much more closely to adults than do the more adventurous males. Sometimes they have a brother who acts for them and from whom they can only be distinguished by being the followers. The brother-sister combination in the *Harry* books is a good example. Sometimes they are mere appendages to adults, holding hands when out shopping. The girl child in *Everybody Said No* occupies the story by washing her doll, knits new pink socks for the doll, sews a new shirt for the doll and dances with the doll. The male child of *I Bet I Could* fantasises a present for his sister, a "house of creamy cake... for best of all she likes to bake". The only girl in *The Winter Bear* makes a posy of winter flowers, another suitable occupation for young females, a group of ghastly non-persons.

Adult females are a little more interesting, their main function being to act as mothers. Many wear aprons and they cook and serve meals: they decorate (*Not Now Bernard*), spend "hours with flowers" (*I Wish I Could*), spoil kids' fun by defending their clean homes (*I Wish I had Duck Feet*), baby-sit (*Bears In The Night*), forage for food (*Are You My Mother?*), and care for babies (*Emily's A Guzzleguts, Emma's Baby Brother*). The only females seen working out of their homes are teachers, freelance witches and the occasional cook.

Mostly they do all this cheerfully and with little sign of strain. They are more likely to show alarm than anger and may have an air of martyrdom. The mother of a new-born baby in *Emily's A Guzzleguts* finally gives way to severe pressure with a suffering look, an arm across her face and a cry of "Oh, James, you are naughty!" After hours of nagging at her, James has climbed fully-clothed into the baby's bath. This is supposed to be a realistic story of the traumas of sibling jealousy, but real parental anger is not permitted. These adult females are a terrified lot. They are often riddled with guilt, as in *Weather Witch* where the witch can have no expiation unless she acknowledges her guilt burden. They are afraid of small animals and insects (*When Willie Went To The Wedding, Fourteen Rats and a Ratcatcher*). They are no good at coping with crises; they scream and faint. They even find children's tantrums hard to deal with: Topsy and Tim's mother allows father to take over when Tim won't wear his wellies. Nor are these women too bright, rarely showing enterprise in solving problems, often causing them by their own stupidity. The cheerful witch, Meg, has *all* her spells go wrong. Mrs. Bird in *The Bird's Nest* nearly causes her own and her husband's demise by a fruitless search for a better nest.

The biased and unbalanced picture of the world viewed through these picture books needs some correction. But it would be just as damaging and false to swing to the other extreme. Many small children do have their mothers caring for them in similar ways to the mother in *Emily's A Guzzleguts*. If picture books portrayed all women as weightlifters or bus drivers, that would be silly, but we could all benefit from a wider and more realistic view of women's roles.

Balancing the books

Amongst the fifty picture books there was some pleasing evidence that publishers and authors are at last beginning to listen to the criticism of the glaring sex-stereotyping in many books for young children. It seems worth looking at them in some detail, since they can begin to provide the balance that we are searching for.

They were nine in number. Perhaps significantly four were without text, thus avoiding the linguistic difficulties. Two, *Sunshine* and *Moonlight*, were by the same artist. The central character in both is a girl child. In *Sunshine* she wakes early, helps her father to make breakfast, is helped to dress for school (but managed most of it herself) and leaves with her smartly-dressed mother to begin a new day. In spite of the lack of text to establish her, she is a real person, pointing out that the toast is burning and reminding her parents of the time. Her father is shown in a caring companionable role, her mother is served breakfast in bed and takes over the care of the child only when father leaves the house. Further, mother is clearly on her way out of the house, rather than being imprisoned within it. *Moonlight* is the complementary story of the end of the day: dinner is followed by the child making boats from melon skins and playing with them in the bath: father washes the dishes and gives his child a cuddle. Her mother then reads to her and she eventually falls asleep. A middle-class picture, but a much more honest and open one than in many books.

The Baby's Catalogue by Janet and Alan Ahlberg is a book in which the headings are the only text. Based on the well-known interest very young children have in "Mothercare" and other such catalogues, it seeks to provide a material for talk. The babies in the book are dressed in unisex clothes and include a black child and twins. The book works through a baby's day. Fathers are shown sharing in the physical care of their babies; mothers are doing other things as well as feeding, washing and comforting. One is shown smartly-dressed on her way to work with a briefcase and a handbag. There is no suggestion that certain kinds of work or other activities are more appropriate to one sex than to another, and adults are seen resting according to their needs.

Two of the Emma books by Gunbulle Wolde, originally published in Scandinavia, have the resourceful Emma in short episodes which show her to be an individual. In *Emma Quite Contrary* she refuses to dress properly, has a tantrum about blocks, enjoys getting dirty, is not pleased with her brother, and refuses to settle at night. In *Emma's First Day At Nursery School* she is at first a little shy, but chooses one of the more boisterous activities, meets her male nursery teacher and makes friends with another girl, with whom she goes off to shout and jump. Daisy in *Demon Daisy's Dreadful Week* is likewise an individual who has her own ideas, culminating in the spilling of yellow paint on the stairs which party children then tread all over the house. The end is interesting. Mother cuddles Daisy; she doesn't like things Daisy does, but she still loves Daisy. Is there a suggestion here that girls have to be fiends to be noticed?

Two books about different kinds of families were in the group of texts selected. *My Family* by Felicity Sen has as its central character a Chinese girl whose father is her only parent. This is a family pattern that is increasingly met with by young children, and it matters that it should be represented in literature: children in this book are seen to be taking responsibility for themselves. In *Lucy and Tom's Christmas* the kind of family that has children, two parents, and accessible relatives celebrates Christmas. Lucy is not a cipher, and there is shared caring between the parents.

The female cat of *The Patchwork Cat* is an entirely convincing

Alice in Genderland

character, who though frightened, cold and tired defends her beloved bit of patchwork quilt from the rats on the council tip. Unlike the gormless Mog in *Mog's Christmas*, she is determined and courageous. With a little help from her friend the milkman she even finds her way home.

It is cheering to report that, in fifty books selected by children most frequently for their own reading, this number should make obvious efforts to present material in a non-stereotyped way: such books are appearing in increasing numbers and improving quality.

Teachers can become more aware of the importance of providing such texts and can be helped by checklists of choice criteria, even if these are used only to stimulate their own thinking. It is also possible to discuss, even with very young children, the existing biased material. Through such discussion they and adults might come to a greater awareness of the degree of match between their picture of the world and that they receive through picture books. One valuable outcome might be the production of their own picture books by the children and their teachers.

Fifty favourite picture books: a 39 place nursery.

Mog's Mumps	Jan Pienkowski	Hamish Hamilton
Meg at Sea	Jan Pienkowski	Hamish Hamilton
The Very Hungry Caterpillar	Eric Carle	Heinemann
Where The Wild Things Are	Maurice Sendak	Bodley Head
In The Night Kitchen	Maurice Sendak	Bodley Head
Harry the Dirty Dog	Gene Zion	Bodley Head
No Roses for Harry	Gene Zion	Bodley Head
The Plant Sitter	Gene Zion	Bodley Head
Twelve Cats for Christmas	Martin Leman	Pelham Books
If At First You Do Not See...	Ruth Brown	Anderson Press
A Dark, Dark, Tale	Ruth Brown	Anderson Press
Weather Witch	Joanna Stubbs	Andre Deutsch
One Eyed Jake	Pat Hutchins	Bodley Head
Lucy and Tom's Christmas	Shirley Hughes	Gollanz
Dear Zoo	Rod Campbell	Abelard
Teddy's First Christmas	Amanda Davidson	Collins
Sunshine	Jan Ormerod	Kestrel
Moonlight	Jan Ormerod	Kestrel
Green Eggs and Ham	Dr. Seuss	Collins Beginner
The Best Nest	P.D. Eastman	Collins Beginner
The Winter Bear	Ruth Craft	Collins
Everybody Said No	Sheila Lavalle	Black

I Wish that I Had Duck Feet	Theo Le Siez	Collins Beginner
When Willy Went To The Wedding	Judith Kerr	Collins
The Bear's Toothache	David McPhail	Andre Deutsch
The Patchwork Cat	Nicola Bailey William Mayne	Cape
Emily's a Guzzleguts	J.J. Strong	Evans
I Bet I Could...	Peggy Blakely	Black
The Baby's Catalogue	A. & J. Ahlberg	Kestrel
Not Now Bernard	David McKee	Anderson Press
Where's Spot	Eric Hill	Heinemann
Run, Run, Chase The Sun	Sugito Hyman	Evans
James and the Model Aeroplane	Peggy Blakely	Black
Atkil's Bicycle Ride	Inga Moore	Oxford
The Big Orange Thing	Jerry Juhl	Andre Deutsch
Bears in the Night	S. Berenstein	Collins Beginner
Fourteen Rats and a Rat-catcher	Tamasin Cole	Black
My Family	Felicity Sen	Bodley Head
King Rollo and the Dishes	David McKee	Anderson Press
Miffy in the Snow	Dick Bruna	Methuen
Emma's Baby Brother	Gunilla Wold	Hodder and Stoughton
Emma Quite Contrary	Gunilla Wold	Hodder and Stoughton
Emma's First Day At Nursery School	Gunilla Wold	Hodder and Stoughton
Topsy and Tim's Monday Book	J. & G. Adamson	Blackie
The Kitten Who Couldn't Get Down	Helen Piers	Methuen
Mog's Christmas	Judith Kerr	Picture Lions
Demon Daisy's Dreadful Week	Phillida Gili	Julia MacRae
Dinner Time	Jan Pienkowski	Gallery Five
Creepy Castle	John S. Goodhall	MacMillan
Rosie's Walk	Pat Hutchins	Bodley Head

Choosing books for young children: maintaining a balance

These notes do not aim to be censorious or prescriptive. They are meant as a practical aid to personal choice. They can be applied to fiction and to non-fiction.

What positive attitudes does this book present to children about the lives of women?

Is there a reasonable balance of females and males?
Are females equally important as males as protagonists?
Are women shown at work outside the home?
Are they in managerial roles?
Are women shown to be enjoying work outside the home?
Are girls in school shown as clever, competent, taking part in a wide range of earning?
Are girls shown as capable of rejecting role stereotypes in play?

Alice in Genderland

Are females at home shown as giving and receiving care and taking a full share of responsibility for all tasks?
Are females and males shown as co-operating with each other towards a common end?
Are females shown as:

> active/enterprising/capable
> courageous/undertaking leadership
> accepting responsibility for a wide range of tasks
> meeting difficulties calmly/intelligent
> unpreoccupied with their physical appearance/cheerful?

What positive attitudes does this book present to children about the lives of men?

If there is a preponderance of male charcters, is there some artistic justification?
Do male and female characters contribute equally to the development of the story or to the presentation of the information?
Is the role of men at work de-mystified?
Are men shown to be doing and enjoying work in the home?
Are men shown to be taking responsibility for a wide range of tasks in the home?
Are men shown to be giving and receiving care?
Are boys in school shown as clever, competent, taking part in a wide range of learning?
Are boys shown as capable of rejecting role stereotypes in play?
Are males shown as co-operating with females towards a common end?
Are males shown as:

> gentle/caring/cheerful/intelligent
> occasionally following rather than leading
> meeting difficulties calmly
> enterprising/courageous without aggression
> sensitive/expressing their feelings honestly
> accepting responsibility for a wide range of tasks
> concerned with personal appearance to some extent?

General book provision: does it match where we live now?

How far does the book collection as a whole offer a fair and balanced reflection of the world in which children are growing up? How many fathers are at work? How many mothers are at home? What is the variety of classes, cultures and colour? What purchases might help correct the balance? What materials could be made by nursery children, their adults and older children to offer perspectives that are close to home?

Literature and Sex-Bias in the Secondary School English Curriculum

Bridget Baines

"He's dreaming now," said Tweedledee: "and what do you think he's dreaming about?"
Alice said, "Nobody can guess that."
"Why, about you!" Tweedledee exclaimed, clapping his hands triumphantly. "And if he left off dreaming about you, where do you suppose you'd be?"
"Where I am now, of course," said Alice.
"Not you!" Tweedledee retorted contemptuously.
"You'd be nowhere. Why, you're only a sort of thing in his dream!"

Alice in Genderland

This article is an examination of the classroom literature presented to children and the effect these books have on the children's view of literature and their own self image.

The roles in which males and females are presented in the novels read, (when women *do* appear at all), confirm the narrow range of activities and careers open to girls, and the lack of sensitivity allowed to boys. The creative relation between reader and story is explored and the article suggests ways in which English teachers can go about reversing the negative views demonstrated in so many of the books on classroom shelves, and encourage reading and writing which also reflect girls' and women's experience.

Literature and Sex Bias in the Secondary School English Curriculum

"I'm not reading that — it's a girls' book" is a complaint that is probably fairly familiar to most secondary school English teachers. It may refer to examples of a wide range of reading, most obviously to the pony-and-boarding-school or nursing-and-romance type of story, but is sometimes extended to any book with a girl as a main character, even though there may be boys as main characters also.

Since the recent upsurge of a range of high quality children's fiction, most teachers would probably subscribe to the view that a book of quality will appeal to boys and girls alike. In addition to the possibility that children may not agree with it, this view seems to have obscured the fact that much of the fiction used in schools does not cater for the interests and needs of girls.

The matter of "interest" was brought to my attention initially by a group of third-year girls in a comprehensive school who asked why they always had to read books about boys (they did not say "boys' books", which they saw as having an additional bias of subject matter, for example, towards boys' sports or war). I challenged this, naming books about both sexes read with me in their first year, when I had also taught them English; they replied that this was so, but that since then they had never been given any book with girls in, and now I was offering them *The Guardians* and *Animal Farm*. While they didn't object to the stories, which they had enjoyed, they said they felt fed up with reading about boys all the time. I said that I'd see what I could do, but I already knew that the novels allocated me by the Head of Department for that group left me little choice. They were: *Moonfleet* by J.M. Faulkner, *The Guardians* by J. Christopher and *Old Mali and the Boy* by D.R. Sherman, and I had added *Animal Farm* by Orwell and *The Red Pony* by Steinbeck for good measure, being enabled to do so by the storage of unallocated stock in my cupboard. All of these are good books in their ways, but girls are scarce on their pages except in the occasional supporting role of sister or mother — even in *Animal Farm* the animals are almost solely male except for a couple of mares, one of whom defects to the capitalist farmers, lured with sugar and the promise of ribbons in her mane!

My first action was to view the stockshelves and stockbook with a new set of criteria, looking for books that might redress the balance — even if I had to "trade" for them with another teacher. There was only *Jane Eyre*, which I thought they might find hard going. No other book in the whole of the third-year stock had even one major female character — girls and women might almost not have existed.

While planning a "compensation programme", using short stories and other materials, I decided to see how many others in the class were in the similar situation of having had such a solidly

Alice in Genderland

masculine-biased reading list. Knowing that every class was provided with groups of books in six-copy packs, as well as a "set book", I decided to find out what they had read during their first seven terms at the school (we were then beginning the eighth).

I asked every member of the class to write down the titles of six "whole-class" novels read since arriving at the school; and below that any other fiction read individually but provided by the school for classroom use (including fiction taken out of the school library). As I had read all of those that pupils mentioned in the first category, I was able to tabulate the sex of the main characters in them — see below.

Boys in Class	Sex of main characters & numbers of books read			Girls in Class	Sex of main characters & numbers of books read		
	+	/	+/		+	/	+/
1		4	1	1		3	2
2		4	1	2		4	2
3		3	2	3		4	3
4		5	1	4		4	2
5		4	1	5		6	0
6		5	1	6		6	0
7		5	2	7		4	2
8		5	1	8		4	1
9		5	1	9		4	1
10		5	2	10		3	1
11		4	1	11		4	3
12		5	2	12		3	1
13		6	0	13		4	1
				14		4	2
				15		4	2
				16		4	2

Key: + = female
/ = male

The blank column speaks for itself.

The titles, and sex of the main characters, are as follows:
The Otterbury Incident	—C. Day Lewis	/
The Boy Who Was Afraid	—Armstrong Sperry	/
The Railway Children	—E. Nesbit	+/
The Magician's Nephew	—C.S. Lewis	+/
Smith	—Leon Garfield	/
Devil-in-the-Fog	—Leon Garfield	/
The Goalkeeper's Revenge	—Bill Naughton	/(+)
Stig of the Dump	—Clive King	/(+)
The Guardians	—John Christopher	/
Animal Farm	—George Orwell	/

Literature and Sex Bias in the Secondary School English Curriculum

At best, a couple of titles had been provided containing a mixed cast — *The Railway Children* and *The Magician's Nephew*. A few of the girls had read library books featuring girl protagonists, but even these had been few (15 books from 16 girls) and were mostly of the pony-and-boarding-school type. Girls had also read more with mixed casts and mainly male characters, so their own reading tended to be across the board to some extent. Boys had read only those with male characters, with the exception of one who had read another C.S. Lewis.

A few pupils had moved in from different classes and in one case, a different school; all but one had read *Stig of the Dump* and *The Otterbury Incident* instead of the two mixed cast stories.

It is also worth considering what sort of minor female characters there are when they do appear in books otherwise male-dominated. Out of the five titles, *The Boy Who Was Afraid, The Otterbury Incident, Stig of the Dump, The Goalkeeper's Revenge* and *Smith* read by one of my pupils in her first four terms at the school, there is little portrayal of girls or women except as a distant mother, or a sister to be escaped from with haste. (*The Otterbury Incident*, and to some extent *Stig* which I did not class as a truly mixed cast story, although it moves towards being one in the last chapter; Lou is, in the mian, given the role of the tiresome sister and the action is seen through Barney's eyes). In most of these stories, as in many others, women are the providers of food and other domestic comforts (the "cult of the apron"). They may also interrupt the adventure, by prohibitions if they are mothers or by being in the way if they are sisters. Sometimes they are more positive in their presence, but may then become harridans or nagging wives, with an undertone of "witch" — as in *"A Bit of Bread and Jam"*, from *The Goalkeepers Revenge*. The most sympathetic and positive portrayal of a woman in the five books is Annie, in *"The Haircut" (The Goalkeeper's Revenge)*, who clearly knows her own mind and can manage both her business and her relationship with her husband, although she does leave a customer sitting half-shaved while she deals with a "domestic problem".

In these as in other books, too few varieties of identity, activity or characteristic are suggested for either sex; for the most part, boys and men are brave and fearless, clever and often aggressive, girls and women are domestic and dependent. For the former, sensitive reactions or shows of feeling are unacceptable; for the latter they are expected. Although these elements may not appear very serious when taken individually, it is the totality of the picture that alarms, especially if earlier and later material is similar.

From some of the studies published in the last ten years, it seems that the features that concerned me are more general than my small sample might at first suggest. Suzanne Czaplinski

49

(1972), and Lenore J. Weitzman et al. (1972) carried out some studies of picture-books that had won the Caldecott medal. The winners over the previous five years showed 261 pictures of males to 23 of females, a ratio of 11:1 which increased to 95:1 when they included animals with obvious identities. A study of Newbury Award winners showed similar ratios, as did Lobban's work on 9 British reading schemes (1974). This also showed a narrow range of careers and very passive activities for girls as compared with boys.

Glenys Lobban's analysis shows that the covert messages on image (the passive domesticated girl; the active, often aggressive boy) are repeated too often to be ignored. The books read by my older pupils in the main conveyed similar images, and though small the list consists of books very commonly bought for schools, having been in print in school editions for some years.

A look at the others on educational publishers' lists shows little or nothing that is very different in this respect, although publishers who have a wider market in mind than teachers' orders for "set books" have begun to show a little more awareness in their choices of new books for publication. However, while there is still such a dearth of well-written, enjoyable books with positive images of girls as well as boys, teachers should not be surprised if female pupils continue to show a preference for the pony and boarding school books, which do have active female main characters who make their own decisions and have their own adventures.

While reflecting on these matters I find myself wondering, too, whether we are only talking of preferences. Leaving aside the argument over whether or not English teachers should use "set books" in the pre-examination course years, those that do would not expect every person in the class to enjoy the set books to an equal degree, so there must be other rationale for using them. One of these, the "Literary Heritage" argument, seems rather unconvincing when applied to my pupils' list, with the exception perhaps of *Animal Farm*. Another series of arguments is provided by studies of readers' psychological responses to literature, which in the last ten years or so have begun to influence teachers' views on why pupils should read (other than for the purpose of acquiring the skill) and have begun to provide fresh criteria for judging fiction. Articles such as those found in *The Cool Web* have increased in number and even where teachers have not read many of them, they may still have an influence through initial and in-service training.

Attempts at analysis of the reading processes have had to concentrate on the readers and the individual portmanteau of images, experiences and perceptions that each uses to create an individual pattern of meanings out of the story being read. While much of this pattern may be shared, in common with other readers in our culture, the individual's private patterning and extension of meanings and images are thought to be of major importance. Actual research on this is still scant because of the obvious difficulties of gaining access to individual imagery and symbolic meanings; such has been our previous literary training, too, that this way of reading has been seen as at best irrelevant and at worst incorrect or mistaken, thereby not acquiring the academic seals of approval.

Norman Holland (1975) studied in detail the responses of five students during and after reading a short story; his book examines not only their richly varied understandings at a range of levels both stated and implied, but also the continual re-creation of the story and its imagery that took place for each person. He observed how personal styles, experience and perception provided a "frame" through which the story was seen, and through which aspects of it were highlighted or related to one another in different ways for each reader. He also observed what he considered to be unmistakable traces of subconsciously symbolic imagery which influenced the "creative relation" between reader and story. This can be a two-way traffic; such images formed by a combination of story and reader may then be retained as part of the person's continuing symbolic world.

It was also clear to Holland that many of the images described by the students were not just "mind-pictures" but held emotional associations sometimes of considerable intensity, which seemed to influence their degree of personal involvement with the story.

Such features are of further interest when combined with the findings of Squire (1964) who notes that the adolescents in his study showed considerable evidence of association and empathy with characters as well as the desire to interpret and judge aspects of the stories; and who observed a correlation between emotional involvement with a story and the formulation of literary judgements. Thus it is clear that we are dealing with complex mental and emotional activities central to the concerns of the English teacher.

In what ways, then, might such processes be affected in female readers' responses to stories about males, which revolve around masculine activities and images, and either exclude females or confine them to limited, inferior or inactive roles? How are females' perceptions of literature affected, and what happens to their individual development of symbolic imagery? What, too, are the cumulative effects on boys and men when these reading and image-making processes take place in response to literature which, unlike the "real" world, is populated so exclusively by the masculine? Some of the possible answers to these questions are disquieting, especially if such deep psychological levels are implicated, as Holland, Squire and others suggest.

With these matters in mind I turned to Bruno Bettelheim's *The Uses of Enchantment*, where his summary of what a story must do to hold a child's interest and "enrich his life" seemed to clinch the arguments for me (although I had to consciously re-apply his views to girls because of his continual use of the masculine pronoun, which though intended to be generic is not truly so, as most of his examples are specifically masculine):

> (The story) must at one and the same time relate to all aspects of his personality — and this without ever belittling but, on the contrary, giving full credence to the seriousness of the child's predicaments, while simultaneously promoting confidence in himself and in his future. (Bettelheim, 1978)

It seems to me that this statement relates directly to the topic of girls' needs in literature. Stereotypes *are* "belittling", especially if they are the only representations of females present; books solely about boys do *not* give "full credence" to the "seriousness" of girls' "predicaments",; and consequently their confidence in themselves and their futures is not promoted.

This matter of confidence is not easy to prove. However, a study which provides the parallel of racialism looked at the portrayal of ethnic minority groups in literature and found considerable positive psychological effects, particularly on self-image, when children of ethnic minorities were given stories about their own ethnic groups. The results were "sufficient to warrant the inclusion of such material in readers for non-Caucasian children". (John and Berney, 1967, reported in Purves and Beach 1972).

My own female pupils perhaps demonstrated a limited self image when, during the course of a discussion as to why so few of them wrote about girls except in autobiographical stories, some said that stories with real action, or about sport, were better when they were about boys (this from a group of girls particularly keen on sport). They also said that girls were not as clever as boys. Were these perhaps reflections of their responses to the mass of literature already encountered, which endorses some activities and experiences as being worthy to explore in literary forms and excludes others? This may become a more acute problem for academically orientated pupils higher up the secondary school, where the ranks of exam-endorsed good authors and literary works contain very few women. One might easily conclude from this that "the proper study of mankind is man".

So what can the teacher do? At the very least a patch-up job

Literature and Sex Bias in the Secondary School English Curriculum

should be done. A booklist similar to that which my pupils had could be improved immediately by the addition of book titles and short stories providing more varied images. For those lower down the school some immediate benefit could be gained by more careful allocation of the first and second-year stock, which may contain more good books with a mixed cast. The insertion of a few new titles over the following year or so would not be beyond the financial limitations of most English departments, especially if such books were used in a positive way, perhaps by the use of comparison, additional back-up resources, discussion of the implications of values presented and by making explicit other possible viewpoints or value positions. Such action would be particularly important when using material already to hand — a necessity, as no school could afford to discard large quantities of bookstock and resources overnight. Discussion of old material in a new light, the use of more diversely characterized short stories and extracts, would also be examples of starting where one can, and was in fact what I had to do with my third-year group mentioned earlier. Far-reaching effects might be gained by a spate of letters to exam boards, pointing out the possible effects of such omissions and suggesting suitable titles for inclusion in syllabi, possibly with sample exam questions as well.

Such action implies a change not just in what books are provided but in qualities of the work encouraged and explored by teacher and class. It means that the world and experience of women and girls then becomes part of the literary experience; that empathy, imagination and "identification" are called into play in relation to both sexes; that female dignity and quality of life commands consideration equally with the male. Only thus can the English curriculum genuinely attempt to serve the needs of male and female pupils.

Stories to Grow On: A re-examination of fiction in the first years of Secondary School

Elaine Millard

"I quite agree with you," said the Duchess; "and the moral of that is — 'be what you would seem to be' — or if you'd like it put more simply — 'Never imagine yourself not to be otherwise than what it might appear to others that what you were or might have been was not otherwise than what you had been would have appeared to them to be otherwise.'"
"I think I should understand that better," Alice said very politely, "if I had it written down: but I can't quite follow it as you say it."

Alice in Genderland

This paper has two main concerns. First of all I examine the kinds of reading experience offered to me and my contemporaries in school and offer suggestions about the sort of stories teachers in today's comprehensive schools should be concerned to offer mixed classes.

Secondly I consider how issues concerning gender, role and stereotyping can be worked into the English curriculum so that the topic is seen not as a single item to be pigeon-holed and forgotten but as an on-going concern which involves all aspects of learning.

I have been using work diaries with my classes (you can read an account of this in *English in Education,* Summer 1983) and have found this a useful way of following up comments and suggestions raised by individuals. The work I describe on stereotyping arose from a chance entry in such a journal, that *Private, Keep Out*, a story by Gwen Grant, was a girls' book.

What criteria do you use when choosing stories to share with your pupils? By this I do not mean books intended for class libraries, to be borrowed for private reading, but those few, special enough to be offered to a whole class. Such books are cornerstones on which I build my teaching, providing the stimulus not only for much responsive and creative writing but also the starting points for small group talk and class discussion. With such books I hope to engage the interest of each child in the class, holding it for an extended period, perhaps over several weeks. Before I introduce a new book to the class I will have read several stories very carefully, trying to match the authors' concerns to the age, abilities and current interests or preoccupations of that group. This selection process is particularly important when considering the needs of the youngest age groups.

Books chosen to be read in the first years of the secondary school play an important role in shaping expectations of what the nature of the subject called "English" will be. In primary schools stories are usually read within the context of the whole school day. They may arise as easily out of an interest in a science topic or as a history project, as from reading or writing lessons. Fiction is not confined there to special areas of the timetable labelled English and can be as varied and many-faceted as life itself. In the secondary school, however, fiction will almost certainly only be sanctioned by English lessons where it will become weighted with that added authority of cultural approval we reserve for the works called "Literature". The stories that people offer one another reflect shared values and prejudices. When such stories are presented in schools in the context of literature these values and prejudices are invested with authority. Stories offer their readers windows onto other worlds, where alternative interpretations of the truth of human experience and new possibilities for explorations are presented; journeys of discovery and role models proposed; as well as escape through enchantment and fantasy. Each of us is as shaped by the ficotional alternative created for us, whether it be by books or other media, as by our lived experience. D.W. Harding has described this process in an essay included in *The Cool Web*, the collection of enquiries into children's reading. He uses the metaphor "spectator" for the reader, whom he describes as someone listening to gossip, or a good story, who enters into a pact with the story-teller, agreeing that what is to be told deserves a hearing. Writers of fiction are privileged in that by holding the reader's attention through their narratives they are able to change their evaluations of the truth of human experience. In the same essay, Harding further suggests that the role of the observer/reader is as important as that of the participant because it allows for reflection. He writes:

Detached and distanced evaluation is sometimes sharper for avoiding the blurrings and buffetings that participant action brings, and the spectator often sees the events in a broader context that the participant can tolerate.

James Britton employs the same metaphor in his discussion of the kinds of satisfaction offered by story. He explains that in the act of story-making:

> We take up, as it were, the role of spectators; spectators of our own past lives, our imagined lives, other men's lives, impossible events.

Recently, I was vividly reminded of the power experience as given flesh by story, while reading the autobiographical first novel by the American Chinese author Maxine Hong Kingston. In *The Woman Warrior* anecdote and myth, closely observed details and fantasy are threaded together, each having a place in the strands knotted into her life. Of the tales her mother told she writes:

> When we Chinese girls listened to adults talking story, we learned that we failed if we grew up to be wives or slaves. We could be heroines, swords women. Even if she had to rage across all China, a swords woman got even with anyone who hurt her family. Perhaps women were so powerful that they had to have their feet bound.

Maxine calls these tales "stories to grow on". I want to consider the sort of stories we think fit to offer for the growth of our pupils by first examining my own experience.

Recalling my first encounter with the subject called Literature, I am immediately aware of a feeling of renunciation. Arriving at a Girls' Grammar School, in the late fifties, from a small primary class, I was overwhelmed. I had intended a career for myself as a literary figure, convinced of my own powers as a story-teller and buoyed up by the example of my favourite writers, Louisa M. Alcott, Anna Sewell, Mary Norton, and, of course, Enid Blyton. My introduction to Literature was through Malory's *Morte d'Arthur*, retold by Charles Kingsley, Walter Scott's *Ivanhoe* and Robert Louis Stevenson's *Treasure Island*. Poetry lessons presented themselves as "Ballad and Ballad Poems" which as I remember celebrated the heroic deeds of men, and the sad plight of the ladies they forsook for their adventures. Woodenly we stumbled our way through *A Midsummer Night's Dream* whose women, then, seemed interchangably destined for the arms of some equally nondescript lover, while the fairies, male of course, along with the mechanicals, enjoyed all the fun, as well as the best lines. Subtly, through omission, rather than design, I was brought to see Literature as a male province and my own tastes something I needed to be weaned from, unsuitable for a grammar school girl with a serious interest in the subject.

The chasm between my own rather romantic tastes in fiction and the books prescribed by my English teachers widened. None of them thought to recommend *Jane Eyre, Middlemarch* or *Wuthering Heights*, so I became persuaded that only men's writing was the stuff of Literature. I was introduced to David Copperfield, Jim Davies, Lord Jim and Joseph Andrews, Julius Caesar, Macbeth, Hamlet and Milton's Satan. Occasionally a vibrant woman crossed the stage; I remember Joan of Arc, Becky Sharpe and Eustacia Vye, but their ends, predictably, were ill-fated and they had been filtered through the sensibilities of men. The pattern was unbroken at university where a course, centered around major authors included only two women, Jane Austen and Virginia Woolf.

I graduated convinced that the truest portraits of women in English Literature had been created by Lawrence. Marion Glastonbury, in her article for the I.L.E.A. *English Magazine*, No. 9, has described a similar "Pilgrim's Progress". She also took on board, without questioning, the values presented in a traditional English course. She writes of Lawrence:

> For a woman there remained a queer obedience, a blind surrender, the extinction of her female will. Like Lady Chatterly we had a choice. Her tormented modern woman's brain had no rest... If she gave herself to a man it was nothing. At last she could bear the burden of herself no more. She was to be had for the taking.

Encounters with the literature of the English classroom effectively stifled and limited my sense of a female self.

In choosing books for my classes I have consciously worked to redress the balance, actively searching out those stories which offer a wider choice of role to the girls as well as boys. The choice is made more difficult because although most girls passively accept choices that boys make, the boys reject quite vehemently material that they consider girl-centered. Research carried out recently suggests that norms of social behaviour in mixed classes, in and out of the classroom, are largely determined by boys. When a group of my sixth formers visited reception classes to find out what kind of stories five and six-year olds chose to read, preparatory to writing for them, one group reported that the six year-old boys would accept no story about a girl unless she was eaten by a monster in the opening pages.

A book I had chosen for particualr attention with eleven year-olds last year was *The Turbulent Term of Tyke Tiler*. The Tyke of the title is a rumbustious, iconoclastic schoolgirl who champions

Alice in Genderland

the weakest member of the class, defies the headmaster, battles with classmates and whose feats of daring culminate in climbing the school's bell tower, causing it to collapse. Throughout the story, Gene Kemp skilfully avoids the use of personal pronouns when referring to this character and it is only by a coup de theatre in the closing pages that Tyke's name and gender are revealed.

I used this surprise ending as a springboard for examining stereotyped images of both sexes. Why had we accepted that Tyke was a boy when reading the story? On first reading Tyke seemed to me a potent symbol, a heroine in the feminist "Girls are Powerful" tradition. It was not until I read a letter from Susan Turner to her parents inviting them to meet me, that I re-examined assumptions based on my own reading. She had written: "I am gong to ask Mrs. Millard if we can have a book about girls, but the boys would moan."

I questioned the rest of this group and discovered a common assumption that both the writer (Gene) and her heroine (Tyke) were male. On a first reading then, girls are denied a positive feeling of identification which I think the boys are frequently offered in class. The ending is in fact a sleight of hand, a subtle cheat. Worse than that isn't there an implied reading that girls' actions are worth attention only when they are indistinguishable from those of their brothers?

The other female characters in the story slot neatly into accepted stereotypes. Mum looks after the home, and big sis is concerned only with make-up and boyfriends; while the head of the school and Tyke's lively teacher, are male, the student is female as is the ineffectual and weepy Miss B, the infant teacher. There is nothing very new about Tyke Tiler except its ending.

This year I chose *Private Keep Out* by Gwen Grant, as the first story for the new eleven year-olds. The story presents a large close-knit working-class family through the eyes of a ten year-old girl with a very positive outlook. I had also begun using work diaries with this group, to allow everybody an individual voice. This is important in mixed groups where class discussion can be dominated by boys. I followed my usual method of introducing a new story, giving each pupil a copy of the story and asking them to jot down what expectations a first look raised. I read the first chapter and in the last ten minutes of this lesson told them to write their first impressions of the book.

The response of a few boys was immediately negative. Alan's reply was the most hostile:

> About the book, P.K.O. I think it is very boring. If you must read something, read something more interesting. Why can't Mrs. Loughran read the boys a story and you read the girls P.K.O.

In previous years, I would have left it at that. This time, however, I decided here was an issue to explore with the whole class. Alan is a quick, articulate member of the class, capable in open discussion of polarising opinion against any sign of feminine weakness. With his permission, I read out his diary entry asking why Alan should have thought the story unsuitable. Boys who had been non-committal in their diaries were quick to supply the ammunition. "It had a girl's picture on the cover", "the blurb called it a girls' story", "a girl was writing it wasn't she?" I thought it was important to look at the idea of male and female interests more positively, so I changed tack. I asked for activities that they thought girls were more likely to enjoy than boys. I further suggested that the boys should make these suggestions. Hands shot up.

"They play with dolls". "They cry". "They like dancing".

The boys shouted to endorse their favourite stereotype. I next asked the girls to supply a familiar list of boys' actions. This time a response came more slowly. Fiona suggested fighting, but before I could write the word on the board, the boys began calling out their own exaggerated claims to physical fitness and greater endurance. Isn't it odd how the most impressive claims of physical superiority came from the smallest boys of the class? Dale Spender's work has established the way in which teacher time is monopolised by the boys in a class. I had very deliberately to silence the boys, coaxing contributions from the girls.

The class were then asked to decide whether the activities selected were typical of one sex or the other, or attributable equally, marking their decision in their books with the letter *M* for Male, *F* for Female or *B* for Both. I then asked for a show of hands from those in the class who thought the activity was appropriate for them. Prior to asking about "playing with dolls", we established together that a doll could mean any representation of a human being. The results, tabulated by Mark, showed that many boys owned Action Men. Surprisingly, many of the boys discovered that dancing was an activity they enjoyed as a group and most of them were interested in clothes and looking their best; both of these attributes they had assigned to girls. Most surprising of all was that in this particular group more girls enjoyed playing football than boys.

For homework I asked them to think about these results and write a comment in their diaries. In the next lesson some summaries were read out and discussed. Some boys seemed to think that this easy toppling of clearly defined differences meant that in some way they had lost ground. Several tried to claim that a preference for smoking and drinking established their superiority, but this was rejected by not only the girls but most of the boys also. By the end of this second lesson I thought the whole class had a grasp of what stereotyping was and that this enquiry that had been generated by one boy's off-hand dismissal of a book had provoked a lot of interesting and instructive discussion. I hoped that I had edged the class a little way towards D.W. Harding's: "detached and distanced evaluation", and towards thinking more critically about images presented to them in the fiction they chose for themselves.

I want to return to something I quoted earlier from James Britton. He described readers as: "spectators of our past lives, our imagined lives, other *men's* lives..." (my emphasis).

I know that "men" is used in its generic sense and does not exclude me, as a woman reader; however, I do think the quotation serves to demonstrate how easily women readers can slip from view. I want the classes I teach to be more aware than ever that women do write and that their stories can command a general audience. I shall think myself successful if I can present Alan with a *Martha Quest* novel or *Jane Eyre* or *The Woman Warrior* in the fifth year without being asked for something more suitable for the boys.

Mike Torbe, in a lecture first delivered to the Coventry branch of N.A.T.E., sensitively explores the relationships which exist between readers and the books they choose. Explaining what it is that makes some of us turn to literature rather than scientific enquiry for understanding he talks of "a central drive within us" which he describes further as: "a search for satisfying meaning that will offer some echo of a meaning for the life we are leading and see around us. It is a search for patterns of understanding."

Authors pattern out for us what would otherwise be incoherent experience and, through their patterns, tacitly grant permission to follow routes mapped out by their perception of what life means. I want to offer my classes many more womanly patterns to complement the self-assertive adventuring that marked my own first encounters with Literature. Such patterns will offer wider possibilities to each member of the class, especially those who feel constrained by a predominantly male perspective. After all, surely we are not still afraid of Virginia Woolf.

The Contribution of Books
Heather Morris

"Better say nothing at all.
Language is worth a thousand pounds a word."

Alice in Genderland

This paper is a brief outline of some of the ways in which sexism is manifested in and sustained through books; and some of the ways in which this can be countered. Both issues have been more extensively and trenchantly explored elsewhere. It has grown out of my experience working in an educational publishing company; out of my role within that company as Equality Officer for the union; out of my involvement with the Language and Gender Working Party over the past four years.

It is not intended as a comprehensive or even representative view of what is happening in publishing, but is a personal response to my position within that industry. The differences in tone between the original paper and the postscript reflect my changing perceptions of both myself and the issue.

What books (and publishers) cannot do

The Contribution of Books

We all operate within a sexist society, both in and out of schools:

> Sexism is integral to our society, necessary to our system, and advantageous to men. It occurs at every level of experience within schools and serves a purpose. (Marion Scott)

This last point is crucial. Sexism is not just an historical accident, an anachronism which, once it is pointed out, will disappear — too many people have a vested interest in maintaining the status quo, even if they will not admit this directly. To change things needs positive action, and that action is coming largely from women.

Women in education are making an especially important contribution, although any teacher will acknowledge that schools have limited capacity to change pupils' perceptions of the world, and books (the focus of this paper) are only one element in this process. Marion Scott, in her excellent article in *Learning to Lose* (Spender and Elizabeth Sarah, 1980) exposes some of the other factors in the hidden curriculum which reinforce the lesson of women's inferiority: who teaches and how; the context of learning and the learning group; classroom dynamics; subject choice.

Describing the problem

However, to return to books and publishing. If we look at the printed materials available in schools the main manifestations of the problem are:

1. The absence of women —
   the use of the false generic "man"
   male as norm
   male dominated view of history, science, literature
   absence of work about women and by women

2. The limited roles presented —
   the "apron" syndrome (especially in early reading materials)
   emphasis on women as wives and mothers
   narrow selection of occupations represented
   the persistence of stereotypes over reality
   stereotyped abilities/characteristics

3. The derogatory view —
   the use of cliched/offensive jokes and cartoons
   illustrations of women used as decoration
   untrue and distorted statements
   an emphasis on physical description

All these points apply to both text and illustrations and in all areas of the curriculum (see Marion Scott). In English, the problem is obvious in the course books that are produced and in the range of fiction and poetry by and about women which is available.

It is hard to read what is not there. The politics of fiction publishing — what gets accepted, by whom, how it is sold — are outside the scope of this paper, and my experience, but these are obviously crucial questions. I want to turn instead to the sort of materials which are produced specifically for schools.

What can publishers do?

The issue is, of course, not just a question of language. I do not believe that eliminating sexist usage from language would in itself transform the sexist basis of our society, but the ways in which language is used in school books often reinforces rather than challenges prevailing assumptions.

Tackling language is, however, the most obvious way in which publishers can approach the problem. Several companies in the U.S. have issued guidelines for company policy, and some of these have had a wider circulation. The best known are those from McGraw Hill, Scott Foresmann and Macmillan. The American branch of the International Reading Association has produced two checklists for analysing sexist content in elementary readers and children's literature (reproduced in the EOC booklet *Ending Sex Stereotyping in Schools*).

In the U.K. no publisher has yet followed that lead. Longman went some way towards developing a policy but its formal adoption was blocked. The Book Branch of the National Union of Journalists (the Union to which most publishing employees belong) has done most towards producing a U.K. equivalent with its publication in 1982 of the *Non-Sexist Code of Practice for Book Publishing*. This, however, is not yet backed up by any sort of sanction although they are campaigning to have it included in individual House Agreements.

Raising the issue, let alone changing practices, can be an uphill and wearing struggle. Companies are not necessarily sympathetic. Books are published or not largely on economic grounds, and unfortunately sexist content isn't yet a sufficient reason for most people not to buy a book, (though this is changing in the U.S.). Extensive rewriting or re-researching is expensive and time-consuming. It is also often very difficult to edit sexism out because it is present in more than just the unthinking use of male pronouns. What is or is not felt to be acceptable is finally a matter of individual judgement.

Authors too, can be a problem. The bogey of "censorship" is often raised. The Writer's Guild of Great Britain accused the Book Branch *Guidelines* of attempting to establish a "new and direct form of censorship and a barrier to freedom of expression". Interestingly, they did not level the same charge against the *Guidelines* for avoiding racism in books which were issued at the same time. Some forms of censorship are obviously all right, a view which the law itself reflects.

The strength of feeling (usually from aggrieved men) roused on this issue can also be surprising. The following is an extract from correspondence with an author of a book on fishing intended for remedial readers:

Editor

Not only are all your anglers male, but so are the fish, "a perch... *he* likes to live in a cave on *his* own"! Fishing, especially at the younger age-level, isn't an exclusively male activity and two photos and a final sentence are not sufficient recognition of girls' interests. I have marked on a duplicate manuscript all the specifically male references, and if you look through this the extent of the problem will become clearer. I am *not* suggesting that you change all these but there are many places where the issue can easily be avoided. For example, passages can easily by recast in the plural; you can use the neutral word "angler" instead of "fisherman"; fish, at least, can become neutral; "his" can often simply be replaced by "the". I have made suggestions for neutralising passages where possible, more positively you could actually introduce girls into the text.

Author

I was simply amused by your desperate attempts to prove that the book is sexist. Presumably, you would want the solitary, predatory perch to be female, rather than male — particularly in view of the fact that these fish are given to being bad tempered...

The great majority of anglers are men. This is a fact. Therefore, in keeping with normal usage, I referred to them as fishermen. I will not include an artificial number of girls, Asians, Jews or Communists in my books in order to produce a work which middle-class critics can judge to be ethnically sound. I don't subscribe to the idea of censorship whether it be overt or covert. Nor for that matter do I propose jumping through literary hoops in order to assuage your tender sensibilities. What I suggest you do is get down to work and produce your own book and let's see what the kids think of it.

Clearly more is at stake here than simply a question of language! Challenging sexism often means challenging the unthinking basis of someone's view of reality, and that is an unsettling experience.

Women in publishing — what we can do

A great many women work in publishing — the majority at junior and middle levels. As individuals their scope for action is limited. We work in sexist institutions which are governed largely by commercial considerations. We may not have the time or support to make extensive changes to manuscripts, especially if we are not involved until a late stage. The constraints we operate under are the same as those for women everywhere — not enough women at influential policy-making levels, our concern not being taken seriously.

In educational publishing especially, it is vital that this should change. Across the curriculum it should be a condition that textbooks give a fair view of women: that they are represented equally in text and illustrations; that their work is recognised and given value; that their writing is published; that their history is rediscovered; that their experience is recorded; that they are not demeaned, devalued or dismissed. Too often, this does not happen and the more people who protest about it the sooner change will come.

Further thoughts

I wrote this paper with the intention of examining one area of my life where politics and practice interlock quite directly — where there is at least the opportunity of translating convictions into actions. Re-reading it I am surprised and alarmed at how easy and straightforward I've made it seem. How much of my personal sense of frustration, compromise, failure, I've left out for the sake of a clear argument. It is revealing to discover how accepting this as a priority has led to over-simplification, even glibness. The form of the writing — controlled, distanced, impersonal — creates its falsity. It presents sexism as something "out there", in society, in other people — whereas the real struggle is taking place within me. It is not by pointing out the errors of others' ways that we learn, but by recognising the narrowness of our own perceptions.

This can be painful; for example, when it was pointed out to me that a series of 11 covers I had commissioned showed 7 male figures, 3 animals, and only one woman. So much for imagining I had the problem under control. It is easy to be discouraged by this, or to begin to think "Does it matter after all?" When I spent hours searching out photographs of women doing interesting jobs nobody noticed anyway. It is also very easy to give in, often without even a fight. I never challenged the author who included this note in his

Preface:

A slight matter first: these days it is necessary to assure some people that when one uses "he" as a pronoun in place of "the child" so beloved of all who utter on educational matters, one of course means to include girls as well as boys.

There are always other pressures — printers' deadlines, cost, the unspoken rules about not upsetting authors — and it's not difficult to use them as justification. Sometimes it's just a matter of not having enough energy to raise it as an issue, to take on yet again the label of "fanatic". Other times there are more immediate short-term gains (personal relationships at work, career prospects) from not making a fuss. The awareness that this desire to avoid conflict is a part of our conditioning which contributes to our continuing oppression is not always enough to overcome that reluctance. To monitor and reflect upon the implications of our own actions takes time and energy and the impetus needs constant renewal. As individuals we need to be reminded, reassured, persuaded that it *is* important, that it *does* matter. We need the voices of other women telling us it is not trivial, that we are not neurotic or obsessed — because there are pressures all the time persuading us otherwise.

It is easy and restful, for a time, to allow a personal conviction to be submerged under the weight of consensus, to relax into accepting that normal equals right. It is possible to justify this by separating life into areas: there are those where we stand firm, others where compromise is possible, where it's not quite so important. This is probably essential to survive at all but it risks falling into the trap of making exactly those distinctions which feminist analysis has revealed as profoundly dangerous — between private/public, personal/political, unimportant/important.

The failures I am most concerned about are failures to make connections — between a perception and an action, between representation and reality, between process and product, between my situation and that of other women. It is crucial to discover these connections, to make them explicit, and to hold on to them.

I work in what is basically a low-paid service industry, although it is perceived as having more glamour than, for example, the hospital workers. It is an industry in which women outnumber men (Lynne Spender has an interesting theory that this is a symptom of the declining power of the printed word). Women, are, not surprisingly, employed in disproportionate numbers on the lower grades. The terms and conditions which perpetuate this imbalance in most white-collar occupations operate in publishing: we are expected to be able to work unpaid overtime, to be free to travel, to work evenings and weekends. Female graduates who have worked as secretaries are perceived as less skilled than their male counterparts. There is no recognition of the responsibilities of parenting etc.

It is difficult to keep a clear connection between this reality and that of other women more dramatically disadvantaged, and the apparently trivial decision not to bother to replace an illustration, not to write a letter to an author, not to analyse the representation of the sexes in a particular book. But if our politics are ever to mean anything, or change anything this is what matters.

As I said at the beginning, re-reading the paper above, several months later, has made me realise how often my practice falls short of my intentions. This is a gloss on what might otherwise seem pat or self-satisfied. The other, more important, realisation has been that it is only through the support and shared perceptions of a group like the Language and Gender Working Party that I have been enabled to write, indeed to *see* in the first place.

Innocence and Experience
The Politics of Gender and Sexual Harassment.
Valerie Hey

"Who Are You?" said the Caterpillar.
"I... I hardly know, sir, just at present — at least I know who I was when I got up this morning, but I think I must have been changed several times since then".

Alice in Genderland

My article aims to revoke the claim that schools are sexually neutral. It is based on my own experience as a teacher in a comprehensive school and encouraged by the growing number of female teachers and students who are breaking the silence on the question of sexual harassment and oppression.

It asks that male staff too, support female staff and pupils in their fight to challenge oppressive attitudes and practices, providing that response is sensitive to the gender politics involved in forming an equal alliance.

Schools are imagined to be sexless environments: children are viewed as innocent of the corruptions of sexuality. This pre-fall Garden of Eden is then supervised by staff whose codes of behaviour forbid them to act in ways that are 'unprofessional'. In a teachers' manual at a school where I taught, all relationships between pupils and teachers were supposed to be 'professionally above suspicion'. This metaphorical phrase translates as a total ban on sexualised contacts between staff and their pupils. But sexuality cannot be kept out by ideologies, any more than it can be defused by good intentions.

In fact, schools are deeply implicated in the production of particular models of masculinity and femininity that are saturated with sexuality; patterns of being male and being female which are locked into positions of dominance and subordination.

Moreover, given our culture's commitment to constructing gender as its chief category, it would be miraculous if school practices were not also involved in the work. What is surprising, though, is the silence on this involvement. Schools seem strangely innocent about their part in this enterprise. The great justification lies in their reliance on the 'differences' between the sexes which then permit them to treat boys and girls as opposites.

If, on the surface, contradictory results emerge, producing conflicting and confusing messages, particularly for the girls, this should not be taken as the operation of a blind lack of intention, merely as the consequence of the competing ideologies in circulation. For example, most schools operate a gender-differentiated curriculum which pre-supposes that girls' primary responsibility is to service others, be they young babies or 'old babies' (men). At some time or another in the course of her school career a girl will be faced with the options system which asks her to 'choose' between car maintenance and people maintenance (home economics). No prizes for guessing her 'choice'. Most institutions have not seriously tackled the polarities which underpin curriculum arrangements; and they present the outcome, heavily gender marked monopolies of certain subjects, as the 'natural' playing out of real desires. Girls we are told, will indeed be girls.

So at one level we actively encourage girls to see their destiny in terms of domestic self-fulfilment. The problems only start when girls take the message too seriously and follow the logic of this compulsion towards satisfying male needs too literally. They begin to eroticise their appearance, decorating school uniform to subvert its intention of de-sexualising them. The school uniform must be the site of struggle par excellence! Simultaneously therefore, schools incite an expectation which they then attempt to discipline, preferring more manageable expressions of feminin-

Innocence and Experience

ity. It seems that the nearest one is encouraged to be intimate with men is in laundering their handkerchiefs.

These sexual experiments do not go unnoticed by the male 'professionals' and despite public disapproval of incorrect dress, privately in the staff-room they feel totally free to express their 'erotic' reaction to young women. I've lost count of the number of times when male staff audibly 'lusted' after female pupils, whose physical appearance was an understood source of 'excitement'. And as female staff we occupied the same space as our female pupils, both subject to the male stamp of approval. For example, in a staffroom that I occupied, women staff were apparently awarded marks out of ten by the male staff on the basis of our 'attractiveness'. It was OK to be the voyeur of young girls, a 'dirty old man', and male potency needed the constant exercise of this power of appraisal as well. You could demonstrate your masculinity by sexually objectifying every woman you chose to. It is this that I call sexual harassment in its broadest sense. Nor was this form of heterosexual predation confined to the staffroom; indeed, it formed a salient feature of the hidden curriculum, an important aspect of the infrastructure of male/female relations about the school.

Characterising the nuances of these exchanges presents something of a problem and in order to focus on the main theme I will designate the phenomenon as the 'Incredible Hulk' syndrome. I've also lost count of the number of times when 'the Hulk' has come to my 'rescue', swaggering in to assist me, bullying and posturing. Frequently my valuable time has been spent in mopping up the resentment after the Hulk's departure. Not only is this macho style disruptive, it is actually predicated on a contempt for those values usually associated with the feminine; this male mode is all hard edges, controlled, physical, loud, emotionless, and directive. In a school with this ethos any deviation from the male model is interpreted by pupils and colleagues alike as 'soft', a derogatory term denoting both femaleness and incompetence.

It is this incessant power-mongering amongst males that I see as motivating sexual harassment, a struggle for dominance amongst themselves and a concern with consolidating the privileges of male bonding at women's expense. In case this all sounds too abstract I would ask all women teachers to recall an occasion when their energy was taken up at the start of a lesson in coping with a sulky or angry male pupil on the rebound from a macho encounter with the headbanger down the corridor.

It will be claimed that the personal testimony presented here is an exception, the accident of individual biography. This attempt to depoliticise these stories I anticipate, but I believe this type of experience to be the inevitable consequence of a society in which the sexes live in antagonistic relations of dominance and oppression. As Anne Whitbread states in *Learning to Lose* (Spender and Elizabeth Sarah, 1980):

> "Given that we have reason to believe that the manifestation of sexual abuse is probably less contingent upon the dynamics of any one school than on the subordinate position occupied by women as a group in society as a whole, then one can assume that as long as the social context includes *some* men, women will be subjected to sexual assaults of one form or another."

If we as women staff are subject to this alleged 'flattery' and 'chivalrous' assistance, which is a cover for the operation of male power, what might we expect our female pupils to be experiencing?

Feminists have begun to name (or re-name) aspects of male sexuality, as sexual harassment, and in doing so have re-defined the former as a problem. What is now required is for the similar position of girls to be combined with the accounts of staff harassment in an analysis which confronts the operation of patriarchal strategies. I accept that there is a power relation between girls and their female teachers but this fact should not obscure their common oppression in the face of male hostility. Failure to recognise this will simply expose the most vulnerable to further humiliation.

In case you think I overdramatise the problem, listen to this testimony from a girl in a London school:

> It's as if the boys rule us and there's nothing that you can do about it. They get you in the corridors and say, 'How big's your tits?' and start feeling you up. It makes you feel terrible about your body. (Quoted by Bea Campbell — *City Limits* 1982 Dec.)

This blatant sexual terrorism is an extreme manifestation of what I've been referring to as sexual harassment. If this incident had taken place in the street, and the offender were older, it would have been a criminal offence. For further evidence of this kind of molestation read the account in *Spare Rib 131, June 1983* on sexual harassment in schools, compiled by two teachers and some of their girl pupils. I believe that the true extent of this problem will *only* be revealed when the school has legitimated it as a cause for action, for what is the point of complaining if the following 'solution' is offered?

> Two boys had been sent to their housemaster for persistent remarks about the size of a student teacher's breasts. They had been told, "If we can't, you can't." (*Learning to Lose*)

Thus, even in the apparent 'disciplining' of errant male adolescents, patriarchy and a collusive supremacy are reasserted and female sex-objectification and subordination are normalised.

Having shown something of the existence of this form of sexual intimidation I would like in the concluding part of this paper to consider what interventions are necessary to counteract this display of male privilege.

Firstly, let me say that I do not underestimate the degree of resistance to the idea that this situation exists at all. When we attack aspects of male sexuality we go right to the heart of male identity, what a man *is* in this society at the present time. I would further suggest that to raise the issue in a school that has not yet accepted the need for some sort of policy on equal opportunities is actually counter-productive. There has to exist a vocabulary of gender politics already, even if this is no more than a recognition of boys' underachievement in English. To insert a discussion of sexual politics into a school where the E.O.C. is seen as a lesbian conspiracy is going to prove impossible. Instead male reactions will be 'excused' by female behaviour, e.g.:

> Well, if she will wear tight trousers she deserves to get her bum pinched... I've often fancied pinching it myself.
> Quoted in "Beware Women — A Sexist School" *(Teaching London Kids* No. 10.)

I've already mapped out how girls are implicated in the making of a flirtatious femininity — a process to which the school, the family, the media, the pop and entertainment industries all contribute. This is not to leave the matter there — for what girls are doing is responding to, and making something viable out of, the enormously powerful models of femininity that are overshadowing them on all sides.

Whilst I would argue for an active view of girls as working with these ideologies of appropriate gender behaviour, they are not responsible for the terms of the transactions that they conduct with these pressures and with men. No matter what they try to make of an oppressive situation, they cannot transform it, and we should not expect them to be able to construct strong female identities when relations with men are so steeped in subordination to a dominating and potentially violent male sexuality.

It is only when schools have begun to be aware of gender issues that any analysis of sexual behaviour will find the necessary space, let alone support, for its expression. If "equal opportunities" are on the agenda then at least a base line has been drawn, which can be extended to include a critical look at current male practices and at the types of femininity and masculinity current in our society.

And it is this engagement with masculinity as it is presently defined that I see as one of the most crucial tasks of a non-sexist curriculum. There is little point in instituting a full range of "equal opportunities" provision, if we ignore sexist graffiti in our classrooms. No amount of woodwork for girls will be enough to affirm their sense of autonomy, if we do not develop strategies to tackle their objectification in sexist abuse and behaviour.

We cannot turn our eyes away from the persistent assaults on our existence any longer, for what we witness in schools is the continuation of a process begun elsewhere and continued "on the streets". Sexual harassment is only one end of a spectrum of male violence that includes the leers and jeers of street hassles, obscene phone calls, the exhibitionism of flashers, the woman battering, rape and murder. All are rooted in a misogyny so overwhelming as to be experienced as a profound moral shock, once "normal" masculinity is seen politically. I am not saying that these phenomena are based in biological maleness: I am arguing that they are both part of the causes and the consequences of patriarchal gender relations.

As part of the development of anti-sexist initiatives in schools, I should like to see the introduction of self-defence classes for females as a positive step in encouraging the growth of physical autonomy — girls, particularly, need the chance to reclaim their physical selves as powerful and worthy of respect. I would be particularly interested in the inauguration of courses on the lines of Kaleghl Quinn's approach, demonstrated in the Channel 4 series *Stand Your Ground* (also a book of the same name). For her method is to engage with the psychological underpinnings of femininity, to recreate a model of female identity that is not centered on fragility, vulnerability and passivity. This enabling strategy will at the very least strengthen girls' notions of the right to define their own space, and offer them a chance to acquire the self-confidence to operate as independent persons.

Similarly any strategy that encourages female solidarity will have beneficial results for their developing sense of self-esteem and power, whether it be organising girls' days with activities, or plays and discussions designed to focus on gender; all girl classes to encourage the take-up in science and technology: a girls' sex education programme which is not dominated by reproduction, and instead includes concepts such as female desire, and the potentialities of girls' bodies; the establishment of girls' groups; talks and demonstrations by women in non-traditional jobs; and the actual investigation of the girls' own cultures in a positive and accepting way.

I anticipate that there may be other consequences of these policies; that these attempts to undermine the ideologies that mould girls into domestic drudges may help to establish a more self-assertive view of female identity, and prevent the acquiring of a male "breadwinner" from being the main priority.

Feminists have been saying for a long time that the problems outlined here cannot be remedied by providing support to women, for they have to do with male style and male behaviour. What I'm asking is for nothing less than the acceptance of the fact that some aspects of masculinity, as women experience it, present problems for us. One of these manifestations is the hidden oppression of sexual objectification and harassment in schools, and this needs our urgent attention if schools are not to continue to collaborate in the institutionalisation of sexism.

Tampax and Flowers
An Approach to Pastoral Care?
Jan Sargeant

"I never ask advice about growing," Alice said indignantly.
"Too proud?" the other enquired.
Alice felt even more indignant at this suggestion.
"I mean," she said, "that one can't help growing older."

Alice in Genderland

This paper considers two main areas. Firstly, it looks at how women have in the past been directed and channelled into the "pastoral" side of school life as a means of career development; an area which has traditionally offered less status or financial reward than subject heads of department.

Secondly, it examines how the lastest developments, involving men in pastoral care, are changing it from a caring approach towards children into a subject in its own right, with all the limits and bureaucracy of any other subject neatly pigeon-holed in the secondary curriculum.

Tampax and Flowers

Not so many years ago, I made an appointment with my then Head of Department to discuss the possibilities of promotion. At the time I was responsible for lower school English, including the organisation of a liaison system with our numerous "feeder" schools. I felt I deserved a scale point for this but I was advised to move into the pastoral area if I was seeking promotion since this was an area more suitable for a woman to pursue than "academia". My own suggestion that I should return to college to gain further qualifications was bombarded with well-meant comments along the lines of my possible wish to marry, have children, the difficulty of combining a job and a course... the possibilities seemed endless, the problems insurmountable. There seemed nothing for it but to devote myself to pastoral care. After all, if I didn't have the qualifications to be a subject specialist, I had all of the necessities for a people specialist; namely I was a woman and women, as we all know, are expert at recognising and accommodating other people's needs.

The fact that many of the pastoral posts were low status and did not in many cases carry the financial distinction of a scale point, spoke for itself. Yet a number of women had over the years been shunted into these posts as a means of career development. Exactly where the said career developed to was not very clear: in some cases, assistant year tutors on a scale 2, in fewer cases, year tutors on a 3 and in even fewer cases, a deputy headship. In some schools, even now, the woman deputy is still renowned for her ability to gracefully dispense tea, Tampax and sympathy, a role of limited if unstartling clarity. Without the experience of timetabling and curriculum work that the other (male) deptuty undertakes, it is hardly surprising that this is the end of the line for many of those who do make it so far.

The pastoral aspect of education is predominantly a caring approach. In his book on the subject, Ben Morris refers to "the essential caring element" being "that part of each of us that cares for others". Women have therefore in the eyes of many an important role to play. Have not women been for centuries the carers, the enablers, the nurturers, for children and/or men to fall back on? Isn't it logical that women should be the likeliest candidates to compensate pupils for the "incompetent mothers" to whom Michael Marland refers in his book, *Pastoral Care* (Marland, 1979)? In speaking with a number of women teachers I have come to the conclusion that most of them have long been aware that a pupil's learning difficulties might be a result of her problems at home, and generally what those problems were, even before such things as profiles were invented, making it necessary for the information to be written down.

For many women, the pastoral aspect of school life was merely an extension of their domestic role, but then again, it is traditional for knowledge which already exists to be stolen and made a science of, mystified often by a process of language development, as we shall see later. What is now happening is that the pastoral element is being focussed on more and more and as a consequence, is becoming more and more structured. The inroads of bureaucratic patriarchy are making themselves more apparent. In *Educational Institutions: Where Cooperation is called Cheating*, Dale Spender argues, "Stratification is fundamental to the male view... With this basic premise of inequality hierarchies emerge as a logical social arrangement". Many schools are now re-organising their pastoral work into a system, using existing hierarchies and formulating when necessary new ones, basing the actual tutor periods on Active Tutorial Work.

Active Tutorial Work is the coined name for a system of active learning, based on children working together, often in groups, and even actually talking together. The phrase itself and the terminology which now surrounds it can be intimidating for those teachers who have not been on one of the available courses. In fact, a whole web of words and jargonese has developed around the area of Active Tutorial Work, or A.T.W. as it is known to the initiated. The esoteric use of language has long been a tool used in the power games of professionals: those who hold the power are those who understand the terminology. Those who remain ignorant of such terms as "deflecting" (that is fending off pertinent questions by posing another) have no access to the sacred pastoral sanctum and therefore remain powerless and excluded. Such terminology has naturally become a useful weapon in the armoury of interview techniques and it is an unprepared candidate who fails nowadays in an interview for a pastoral post to throw in at least some of the jargon associated with a pastoral syllabus. Never mind the quality of care, feel the width of the coursebook!

The educational ideas associated with Active Tutorial Work are not in themselves new. Some teachers, many of them in English and Drama departments, or Junior and Infant schools, have long practised group work, talking and listening skills, dealing with attitudes and personal and social development. The whole idea of an active learning approach, in which children actually participate in the process of education, is nothing new — to some teachers. Others, however, fail to see the relevance or efficacy of such methods in their particular subject area, or perhaps they are frightened by the potential loss of classroom control in such a participatory situation. Perhaps, even, they are unaware of how to structure such sessions effectively — a very real consideration.

Whatever the reasons, it is necessary and vital for all children to be given such exploratory sessions at some time in their education, and it is perhaps only in their "tutor period" in some schools that such opportunities are made available. For this reason alone, then, Active Tutorial Work can be a valid and valuable area of the school curriculum. At least there is one lesson a week when children can be actively involved in their learning. Then again, if there were less mystification, perhaps more teachers would be willing to use such methods in general day-to-day subject teaching. I see no reason why the skills and relationships fostered in such pastoral work cannot be developed elsewhere, given that a caring approach could be adopted even within the macho confines of a science laboratory. Such developments are now being fostered by the people who run A.T.W. courses but whilst schools are eager and willing to grasp at the lifeboat of a system of developing tutor periods, not many teachers feel easy at the prospect of the methodology being used within their own subject area. Such an approach does, admittedly, threaten the traditional power balance between passive recipient (child/woman) and omniscient subject specialist (teacher/man).

Does the only status it can be afforded have to be based on the rigid patriarchal structure of specialist subjects? And will that subject then adhere to the traditional division of what boys need as opposed to girls? At a course I attended on A.T.W. I was discussing with one teacher the pastoral syllabus at his school. The boys did what he termed a Ph.D. — paper hanging and decorating. The girls did not follow this particular activity. It was not deemed suitable as a "lot of swearing goes on". No doubt the girls acquire instead a B.Sc. — Bachelor of Service and Care?

Perhaps as a result of all this structuring and development, more men are becoming involved in the pastoral side of school life. A number of senior posts are now being held by men and one might assume that this could be a response to men's growing awareness of the skills involved in caring and enabling, for so long the traditional provinces of women. On the other hand, altruism may not be the reason.

Their newly kindled interest may be a response to more pressing needs — in a climate of educational recession and less promotional opportunity within subject areas, the pastoral side of school life may be an appealing route to a further scale point. The pastoral area may also be that much more attractive now that it has been rendered more concrete in form. After all, there is more often than not a syllabus to follow; in many schools, the Year Tutor is seen as a tool for the implementation of discipline, in others, as the career adviser. The "essential caring element" is perhaps too firmly cast in the feminine role for men to pursue this angle, but if there is a systematic approach, concrete objectives and text books to follow, and a scale point at the end of the rainbow, then this area could be very appealing.

Meetings have been held, committees formed, even a National Association founded, all in the name of pastoral education. They all provide a platform for discussion about how pastoral work can be implemented in schools. Yet I see little reason why it should be developed as either a subject on the timetable or as a means of career development for aspiring males. To me and many women, pastoral care is an essential part of the general interaction between any teacher and any pupil in any classroom.

Teacher without a Surname
Margaret Sandra

"What's the use of their having names," said the Gnat, "if they won't answer to them?"
"No use to *them*", said Alice; "but it's useful to the people that name them, I suppose. If not, why do things have names at all?"

Alice in Genderland

In this article Margaret Sandra describes her decision to abandon both her husband's and father's surnames in favour of her two forenames by the apparently simple step of removing her surname by deed poll.

She recounts the obstacles a bureaucratic school system placed in the way of her decision. Her growing feeling, that the place afforded women in society is defined through a patriarchal system of denomination, leads her to affirm that such issues are not trivial but important stages in women's growing struggle for a real identity.

Teacher without a Surname

Having been asked to write about being a teacher without a surname, I need to explain a bit of personal history and ideology.

I dropped my surname/sirename, in February 1978 by deed poll, a remarkably easy process clearly described in Jean Coussins' N.C.C.L. booklet *What's in a Name?* I chose this legalistic method after discovering that official control over naming is remarkably weak. You can change a name by customary use over a period of a year, and in fact I had already operated this when I changed to using my married name in 1968. This change had been treated as absolutely nominal and no obstacles had been created, but I was very aware that dropping all surnaming as against adopting a husband's name, would be treated very differently, so I approached the process with caution.

My interest in naming began early. My sister changed her name from Jane to Jean, by custom, when she was thirteen. Myself: I was obsessed, as most children are, with personal naming and fantasised with more interesting names than Margaret. "Darrell" from Enid Blyton's *Malory Towers* series seemed attractive to me for quite a long time.

Eventually I accepted that Margaret Sandra Chalker was my name and apart from developing clear enunciation and a quick anticipation over questions about spelling, I settled to its use.

My name-debating did raise an issue I might not have perceived until later and that was the dying out of my father's name because he had no sons. This made me feel very sad. I had great love and loyalty for him but the only solution as far as I could understand was to find a man to marry whose name could be double-barrelled with my father's and thus both men's needs could be satisfied.

In the event I didn't and so became Maggie O'Connor on marriage, a name I enjoyed enormously. It was an easy, resonant name which required no spelling instruction! The diminution of my forename I had acquired in my first job when there were three Maggies in the department.

After my divorce seven years later I became increasingly uncomfortable with the form of address, "Mrs". It led people to ask questions about my supposed husband which involved, to my mind, unnecessary explanations about my marital status. The solution was to adopt the feminist mode of address "Ms". This parallels "Mr" insofar as it indicates gender but not marital status. "Mrs" and "Miss" are, after all, signifiers of sexual availability. The former is clearly the property of her "Mr". Thus we have the custom described in etiquette books, of addressing a couple by the husband's name, i.e. Mr and Mrs John Smith (sorry Smith people!). Mrs Smith, however, is still her father's daughter and bears her "maiden" name until rescued by marriage!

Alice in Genderland

It was clear to me that women have a passive role in that process of personal naming. They can influence, or even dictate, the forenames but the surname, the family signifier, passes through the man, totemising patriarchy at every level of our existence.

"Ms", while useful to the definition of women as married or single, has been quite successfully subverted in meaning by misogynists, to be synonymous with other derogatory terms for women like "libber" and "divorcee". (Consider why there is no term in the English language for the man who is divorced!)

When I changed to describing myself as "Ms" in school, it was adopted, on paper at least, very easily. Pupils wrote it on their new exercise books and debated my reasoning. They were curious and mostly supportive though I am very aware that their acceptance lay as much within the power relationship as with their understanding of aiming at parity of meaning between Mr and Ms.

Colleagues were more of a problem. Administrative staff used it punctiliously in written forms but I could hear the discomfort in their tones as they attempted to voice it. We do not normally use words, expressions, etc. until we feel confident about what *we* think they mean so, as I didn't explain my new form of address, their response wasn't surprising. Most teaching colleagues resolved their problem over my form of address by either continuing to refer to me as "Mrs", making jokes about pronouncing "Ms", or avoiding my name altogether and relying on catching my eye!

These responses were not unexpected and I bided my time, hoping that perseverance and tact would be sufficient in the long run. One other problem which occurred to me was how far other colleagues also wished to adopt "Ms" as their form of address. Some I asked; others I addressed on paper according to my feelings at the time, hoping for responses. Those who did express a preference divided evenly between retaining the traditional forms of address and choosing to be called "Ms".

However, relatively few reacted to me personally though I was aware of an increasing climate of antagonism towards those of us on the staff who expressed pro-feminist opinions. This came to a climax at a staff party, where a strongly anti-women statement was made by a departing male colleague. Thus we came to start the following academic year with an equally strong statement in the open staff meeting by the head teacher about equal rights and opportunities. This relaxed a lot of the tension and a women's group began to meet where the specific experience of being female in a mixed comprehensive was explored, and I felt able to explain to a wider audience my motives for changing my name.

The previous year I had come to the decision that whilst "Ms" as an attempt at neutrality was useful in developing people's consciousness, it couldn't solve the fundamental problem of women's powerlessness in the process of naming. Women have no autonomous names. We are limited to conferring forenames and expected to accommodate our own complete name change at least once, nowadays more often, in our lifetime. What does that do to our perception of ourselves? To our ability to control our lives?

The power to define and name is fundamental to understanding and changing the world, yet at the most personal level women are nameless except when identified by their father or husband's surname.

For these reasons I chose to take power for myself and remove my surname by deed poll, thereby claiming my forenames as my total formal name. It was a very exciting day and whilst I've been angered, irritated and amused by a patriarchal society's attempts to undermine my assertion to name myself, I have never regretted it. Refusing a surname exposed very clearly the function it performs within the state to record, catalogue, serial number and retrieve information on individuals. It is not relevant to describe here the two-year battle with bureaucracy to change all my personal documentation. Suffice to say, that if you need to file me, do it under "M".

Having successfully asserted my right with every legal and government department to not have a surname, I felt confident to change names officially in school. Initially this process was delayed by me until I had experienced the worst of the psychological pressure on my identity, since I anticipated that similar pressure in the workplace could have been intolerable. In the event, the changeover in September 1980 was remarkably painless. Much of this I attribute to the calm acceptance and influence of the head teacher and the school administration officer, two women who respected my wishes and defended my right to be taken seriously, without necessarily agreeing with my beliefs. Their official use of my formal name at meetings, and in announcements, and their continued use of my diminutive "Maggie", in personal contact, sustained me and eased considerably the transition to the use of my proper name by colleagues. Inevitably some used the same tactics as with Ms; one, so far unidentified, stole my mail for two terms. I believe there was a definite link between this malicious act, designed to make me appear inefficient and careless, and the relabelling of my letter rack with my new name.

In contrast my classes were enthusiastic. They enjoyed having the apparent right to call me by forenames, a response which opens up the question of school naming as control. "Call me Sir when you speak to me, boy!" I didn't have any sense of my authority being undermined, even though as Head of Faculty I do have a disciplinary role. However, I do appreciate that I made this radic-

Alice in Genderland

al change as an experienced teacher at the top of the school hierarchy, confident of the support of senior colleagues, and that is a pretty safe position in terms of the power relationship with pupils.

"The personal is political". This personal act is one of the outward ways in which I can assert, through my forenames, the right to challenge the male definition of women as property, a challenge which I would want to extend to all assumptions about females and their role in society. It is my contention that we shall not get to the root of girls' underachievement in schools or tackle seriously women's low pay and unemployment, until women can experience the assertion of power. Reclaiming the right to name can be part of that process as those of us who have done it can testify. Then I can hope for the utopia Marge Piercy describes in *Woman on the Edge of Time*, where naming is both individual and collective but never possessive.

Structuring Stereotyping

Pat Barrett

"Would you tell me, please, which way I ought to go from here?"
"That depends a good deal on where you want to get to", said the Cat.
"I don't much care where — " said Alice.
"Then it doesn't matter which way you go", said the Cat.
" — so long as I get somewhere", Alice added as an explanation.
"Oh, you're sure to do that", said the Cat, "if you only walk long enough".

Alice in Genderland

As an Advisor, my job takes me into all areas of Education. I "cover" Nursery to College of Education and visit establishments every day. This makes me an "outsider" in a sense, since I am not involved in the day-to-day organisation. It also enables me to observe and compare in a fairly unique way. This article is a description of what I see but, much more, it is an attempt to outline the basis for the sex-stereotyping I observe and to suggest ways in which the situation might be changed.

Patterns in gender stereotyping

"This E.O.C. booklet suggests that the children should be required to take part in all the activities and not be allowed to do stereotyped things only. What do we do with the idea of choice and free expression?"

This was the worry of an Infant Head, when I visited her school. We went to look at the reception class. The boys were playing with the construction bricks. The girls had aprons on and were washing the dolls' clothes in a tub.

The same issue arose in a secondary school inspection recently. In the option choices no girls did Physics *and* Chemistry and the proportion of girls to boys in Physics groups was one in five. In this same school, the staff were waited on at lunchtime by girls and the coffee served by girls.

Tape-recordings made by teachers for in-service work of small group discussions follow a recognisable pattern. When the group is mixed-sex, the boys disrupt.

There are Comprehensive Schools where seventeen men hold senior positions and only Home Economics and Remedial Departments have female Heads.

In one school a very experienced female was not short-listed for a Head of Department post because the Head wanted a man; the reason given being that the Department was all female.

None of the above is new. It has been documented over and over again, this apparent circle of learned and re-inforced stereotypes. The children enter school with their gender roles ascribed and learned and the curriculum and staffing structures, indeed all the minutiæ of the school day, endorse how they are.

Structure and stereotype

"Structure" is an interesting word. "Lack of structure" is often the worst thing that can be said (and *is* said) of probationer teachers' lessons. Primary school head teachers fear to move away from a structured reading scheme to the use of "real" books. They excuse this with such comments as:

"I like to know how every child is progressing."
"The parents like to know what book their child is on."

The timetable is constructed in comprehensive schools, often with great mystery. In our County we still have primary schools where an elaborate timetable is sellotaped to one of the cupboards in the Head's room, containing such esoteric half hours as

Choral/ Composition/ Mech. Arith./ Spelling/ Hist/ Geog/ Mental (!) There is, clearly, a belief that knowledge and learning can be packaged in this way. There is no room (or time) for negotiation between teacher and pupil. The need for the children to make meaning is unrecognised and the teaching is a one-way process. The product is an examination candidate fit to pass.

This approach to school organisation has differing effects on male and female children and adults. In classrooms I visit, where the school ethos is structured in this way, female probationer teachers fear to move into group discussion or drama, since they recognise that any noise from the classroom will be construed as lack of discipline.

Since this would appear as an endorsement of so-called female "weakness" they are loath to take the risk. Male probationer teachers, on the other hand, who attempt these approaches to work are perceived as "trendy".

In classrooms where the school ethos, timetabling restrictions and available materials demand teacher-centred work, the girls are passive and most of the teacher's time is spent controlling the boys, who disrupt. Many teachers under these circumstances resort to writing tasks, as a method of control, and the children learn to view education as a system where they provide a product which the teacher marks. In such a situation disruptive girls are seen as unnatural, more so than disruptive boys. It is accepted that boys will challenge authority. The teacher's business is to control their behaviour and attempts are made to choose stories, poems and other materials which will appeal to them.

Women teachers, who have taught in girls' schools admit to the difficulty of using *Jane Eyre* or *Pride and Prejudice* in mixed sex classes. "Literature as control" also means that the teachers are forced into the position of handing over their perceptions of the text and discussing in terms of "style", "characterisation" and "authorial background". The girls are deprived of the opportunity to explore their feelings in relation to the issues raised by women writers. All the students are encouraged to regard Literature as a discipline to be learned in much the same way as they learn their Physics formulæ.

In such schools the staff meetings are usually confined to administrative matters. The curriculum structure is regarded as a given, and beyond challenge. School uniform, discipline and organisation are on the agenda. Any attempt at discussing flexibility in these matters is regarded as "soft" or "lax". The female stereotype of weakness and accommodation is unacceptable. The male stereotype of toughness and strength is the prevailing ethos. Women teachers can neither introduce any difference nor endorse the ethos while remaining true to themselves. They are in a double-bind.

Control or Co-operation

Behind all of this attempt to maintain control is fear. Loss of control is loss of power. When the organisation of their own learning is given to the children, the teacher's role is vastly different. In a primary classroom some children were deciding what they needed to know about the history of their own village. They listed their questions such as "What was the school like?", "What were the houses like?", "What games did they play?", "What clothes did they wear?" They then listed all the places or people from which they might get answers, visited the library, asked their teacher for advice and consulted their parents.

The teacher made time for all this, suggested sources, enabled the children to discuss their findings and come to conclusions. Words to describe the teacher's role, a man in this case, would possibly be supportive, enabling, encouraging or fostering. It is no accident that these words are often used to describe female roles. In the same school a female teacher was pursuing the same approach, endorsed by the Headteacher. I have rarely seen such a sense of achievement, as she explained her interest in the skills and confidence which the children were developing in the *process* of pursuing their work. This school has no "English" exercise books. Their resources lie in a large selection of fiction and non-fiction books for the children and staff to use. Staff-room discussions on discipline focus on the importance of involving children in their work.

This school is putting control into the children's hands. It seems to me significant that some of the male members of staff are feeling anxiety. They are used to control from without the person. Their own childhood and adult experience has endorsed the wielding of power. They fear what they may rarely have known, the looking inside to face their own feelings. The women on the staff know what it is like to live many layers within one life. They can hold their own feelings and empathise with the children's need to face challenge and be supported through it. The women have practised this all their lives. They know too that knowledge is not a given truth with defined boundaries. They have lived, most of them, in situations where they are the peace-makers, the enablers of conversation, the listeners. They have negotiated between opposing values. They have lived in a world where male values are enshrined and female perceptions hidden. They have lived at least two sides to every story.

Alice in Genderland

What do stereotypes do to people?

Margaret Sandra's work shows that girls do significantly better than boys at English Literature 'O' Level. At a recent conference in our county, discussion groups felt that this could be attributed to girls' ability and willingness to empathise with the feelings expressed in the writing they are studying. Does a school ethos which emphasises toughness and "hard knowledge" make English at 'A' Level a haven for the girls? Does it deter from English those boys who in a more enabling atmosphere might be encouraged to be truer to themselves and their feelings?

To describe such groups as a "haven" for the girls is a deliberate choice of words. A teacher in another of our primary schools, where needlework is done by the girls and woodwork by the boys (still!) spoke of her pleasure in the time she spent with the girls alone. "They tell you all sorts of things and you learn such a lot about them and their families."

Her description reminded me of the quilt-making groups of old in our county. They were havens of peace and a source of strength to the women in the hard lives of the pit villages. In the next room, where the boys with a man teacher were building their boats and planes and rockets, no such atmosphere prevailed. For the same reason as the primary woman teacher above, I can sympathise with the Home Economics teacher I worked with, whose room was a rest cure for the girls from boys' sexual harassment. This teacher refused to teach mixed-sex classes. She offered H.E. for boys on the option list, giving as her reasons the fact that the boys were behind the girls in their progress. Possibly this was true; girls are expected to work more in the kitchen at home but she was a very capable teacher, adept at mixed ability teaching. I couldn't blame her for her need to have some peaceful lessons, where she could give all her attention to the girls.

Much anxiety is expressed that women teachers remain at the bottom of the promotion ladder. But when women reach the short-list, the interview style often militates against them. Interviews rely heavily on the ability to talk fluently about yourself and your understanding of the work required of you. There is much documentation of the roles ascribed to men and women in mixed-sex talk. Women are, more often than not, ascribed a facilitating role in conversations. If they do express views, they are more frequently interrupted and diffidence is expected of them. In classrooms and staff rooms the ability to facilitate discussion and genuine exchange, however, is an important role to aim for. Interviews usually test the reverse of what is really required.

As Advisor, I see teachers in the classroom. A very articulate, relaxed male whom I know to be dogmatic in the Department and over-charismatic in the classroom is much more plausible at interview than the quiet, firm but gentle female, who I can see is fighting within herself to adopt a projective role. The fact that she is usually more competent in her work is not revealed (at least by her) at interview. The odds *are* stacked against female candidates of this quality. Lack of success on the part of women in the alien situation of an interview is not, however, the chief deterrent to women's applications for jobs.

The majority of women teachers are working in schools organised hierarchically with an ethos of power and control. They see the kinds of qualities which appear to be expected of Heads of Department or Heads of Schools and do not wish to operate within those terms. They shun the role, however, of Senior Mistress, with its dead-end tasks of "flowers, visitors and Tampax".

Most often the role of the Deputy Head is couched in terms of support for a curriculum structure and control model based on stereotype. Many women cannot see themselves in these roles, which are at odds with their identities. They return from courses on "Organisation in the Primary School" (to which they went eagerly with hopes of preparation for promotion) their folders full of outline job descriptions for posts of responsibility, advice on creating centralised resource areas, simulations on how to run a staff meeting, suggested ways of mobilising parents but very little on ways of organising self, staff and resources to provide a climate for learning.

There is a call from some directions for a return to single sex education, either within one institution or separate schools. All my feelings reach towards this. I remember the support and endorsement I had from my much admired teachers in my own girls' grammar school days. I recall the personal learning I have achieved in women's groups and the sense of freedom and strength within them. In a recent Channel Four discussion, Dale Spender and Mary Warnock talked in different ways of women making their own space. Mary Warnock was anxious to "build bridges", to maintain possibilities for woman's advancement in the world as a whole. Dale Spender expressed her delight in writing and researching for women, disregarding the "ghetto" men have created for themselves. In the educational world which reflects so clearly the values of society, it is inappropriate to take up either of these positions. There are important emphases which I have seen women bring to the schools.

It is at some cost to them in anxiety and stress if they are alone in the effort. To adopt an enabling role within an institution which has always relied on hierarchies of power and status to deal with discipline, organisation, classroom role expectations and regards the curriculum as "given", is very stressful at a very personal level. A teacher, a head teacher or a child, needing to work in a *negotiated* framework faces a challenge to their identity when they are expected to live roles at odds with their personal way of life. The new head teacher, faced with a staff who are unused to team discussions and who expect orders from "above", takes on an enormous counselling role for the stress in the staff and is isolated in a new and unpredictable way. We do not provide adequate support networks for these and similar situations.

The problem

The most heartening sight for me is when I visit Infant schools, where reading is seen as a process of introduction to books for enjoyment and there is an air of excitement at the topics of interest developed from the children's own ideas. The most disheartening is to visit one of our smallest schools, where the Headteacher, who taught the few children to read "by the mother's knee method", has now retired. The new Head wants help in buying *Ladybird* books and *Wide Range* "to give the children a sense of progress and a more systematic, structured approach to reading!"

As more junior and infant schools amalgamate (the result of falling rolls) and men are appointed to run the J.M. & I; as we have just appointed our first male Headteacher of an Infant School, as role models disappear for the girls when comprehensive management teams become all male and governors are appointing men "because they have a family to look after", we must, as women, maintain the perspective we have of the classroom, *not* as a "leavening" of the gloom but because enabling, supporting and sustaining are important for the education of all children.

At all points we must try to break the cycle which perpetuates rigidly intellectual ways of knowing, encodes these in strict patterns of timetabling and classroom behaviour and supports them with books and material which enforce stereotyped teacher and pupil roles.

I am sure that all the situations I have described in this article will be recognised by my women friends. My men friends will resent the implication that "open learning" or whatever you may call it, is the prerogative of women. I have tried to make it clear that in schools which are built on gender stereotyped structures men can succeed by acting out traditional roles, if they wish. Women do not have this choice. There are different stresses for men and women. If they choose to act their stereotypes neither men nor women can be honest before the children. In a few schools where these stereotypes and their consequences have been examined and dealt with, gender has become a less dominating issue.

All teachers, advisers, parents, children, ancillary staff or any member of the education community will have differing responses to the circumstances in which they work and particular ways of intervening to break the circle of ascribed roles. It takes great energy, a strong sense of personal identity and the ability to recognise stress-related behaviour to move children, staff, caretakers and colleagues towards more cooperative ways of working. Our management courses, in this county, do not generally tackle these areas. Women and men in leadership roles remain puzzled, anxious and lonely, as they observe themselves over-working, "spinning too many plates in the air" and receiving none of the supportive enabling practices they are providing for the children, their colleagues and parents.

"Coming out" or "standing up to be counted"

This over-working is dangerous as a response. It arises from the need to shift attitudes within a school or L.E.A. almost by emotional will-power. It is, however, change by stealth. It does not make explicit the philosophies behind the push for change. To "make public" the issues behind stereotyping has its own risks. During a long language course for Primary teachers two years ago, I introduced the notion of racism and sexism in children's books. It was only this element of the course which caused a furore from the men and they argued about sexism and not racism.

I pondered on what aspects of their personal lives their discomforts were based. I watched the silent women and knew I had to win a battle for them. It is important to keep this issue raised again and again, in spite of the resulting loneliness. Endorsement of it as a serious issue for debate is still the level at which we have to operate.

We look with excitement at those L.E.A.s where practical policies for change are emerging. I recognise that my interest in this issue is a reflection of my own style and personal need as well as an intellectual conviction. It is a matter of bringing the issue out of the pub, the school corridor or wherever we huddle for sharing of anger and mutual support into the staff meeting. It is more urgent than women's pursuit of status, recognition and promotion. It has got nothing to do with helping men to see the light, which they can do in their own terms. It is about the way in which power is used and abused and it is central to the question of learning.

Bibliography and Further Reading

Children's Books and Books for Older Readers

AUSTEN, Jane, *Pride and Prejudice*, Penguin 1983
BLYTON, E., *First Term at Mallory Towers*, Granada 1983
BRONTE, C., *Jane Eyre*, Penguin 1983
BRONTE, E., *Wuthering Heights*, Penguin 1983
CARROLL, L., *Alice's Adventures in Wonderland* and *Through The Looking Glass*, Puffin 1983
CHRISTOPHER, J., *The Guardians*, Heinemann
DAY LEWIS, C., *The Otterbury Incident*, Puffin
ELIOT, G., *Middlemarch*, Penguin 1983
FAULKNER, J.M., *Moonfleet*, Puffin 1983
GARFIELD, L., *Smith*, Puffin 1974
GARFIELD, L., *Devil-in-the-Fog*, Puffin
GOLDING W., *Lord of the Flies*, Faber
GRANT, G., *Private Keep Out*, Armada
JACOBS, J., *Hereafterthis*, The Bodley Head 1973
KELLOGG, S., *Can I Keep Him?*, Warne 1973
KEMP, G., *The Turbulent Term of Tyke Tiler*, Puffin 1981
KING, C., *Stig of the Dump*, Puffin 1983
KINGSLEY, C., *The Morte d'Arthur*
KINGSTON, M., *The Woman Warrior*, Picador 1981
LESSING, D., *Martha Quest, (Book One of Children of Violence)*, Panther 1977
LEWIS, C.S., *The Magician's Nephew*, Fontana Lions 1983
NAUGHTON, B., *The Goalkeeper's Revenge*, Puffin 1979
NESBIT, E., *The Railway Children*, Armada 1978
ORWELL, G., *Animal Farm*, Penguin 1983
PIERCY, M., *Woman on the Edge of Time*, The Women's Press
PLOWDEN, LADY ET AL. (editorial board) *Famous Writers*, Macdonald Educational 1969
SCOTT, W., *Ivanhoe*, Penguin
SHERMAN, D.R., *Old Mali and the Boy*, Heinemann
SPERRY, A., *The Boy Who Was Afraid*, Heinemann
STEINBECK, J., *The Red Pony*, Piccolo (Pan) 1975
STEVENSON, R.L., *Treasure Island*, Penguin
UDU GAWA, T., *The Little Chick*, Wayland 1978
UNGERER, T., *No Kiss for Mother*, Methuen 1974
WHITE, E.B., *Charlotte's Web*, Puffin 1983

Critical Analyses of Children's Books

BETTELHEIM, B., *The Uses of Enchantment,* Thames & Hudson 1976, and Peregrine books 1978

CHILDREN'S RIGHTS WORKSHOP, *Sexism in Children's Books: Facts, Figures and Guidelines,* Writers and Readers Co-op 1976

CZAPLINSKI, S., *Sexism in Award-winning Picture Books,* extracts from dissertation. In *Sexism in Children's Books,* ed. Children's Rights, 1976 Writers' and Readers' Publ.

DIXON, B., *Catching Them Young: Sex, Race and Class in Children's Fiction,* Pluto 1977

JOHN, V. & BERNEY, T.D., *Analysis of Story Retelling as a Measure of the Effects of Ethnic Content in Stories,* New York: Yeshiva University 1967

LOBBAN, G., *Sexist Bias in Reading Schemes* in *The Politics of Literacy* ed. M. Hoyle Writers and Readers Co-op 1977

LOBBAN, G., *Presentation of Sex Roles in British Reading Schemes* Forum 16(2) Spring 1974 pp. 57-60

LOBBAN, G., *Sex Roles in Reading Schemes in Sexism in Children's Books,* Writers and Readers Publishing Co-operative 1976

MEEK, M., WARLOW, A., & BARTON, G., *The Cool Web,* Bodley Head 1977

PURVES, A.C., & BEACH, R., *Literature and the Reader,* National Council for the Teaching of English 1972

STINTON, J., ed. *Racism and Sexism in Children's Books* Writers and Readers Publishing Co-operative 1979

STONES, R., *Pour Out The Cocoa, Janet: Sexism in Children's Books* Longman 1983

TORBE, M., *Reader, Book and World* (Lecture Notes from Coventry N.A.T.E. 1982)

WEITZMAN, ET AL. *Sex Role Socialisation in Picture Books for Pre-School Children,* in *Sexism in Children's Books,* 1975 op.cit.

ZIMET, S., *Print and Prejudice,* Hodder and Stoughton 1976

Children Reading, Writing and Learning

ASHTON-WARNER, S., *Teacher,* Virago

ASHTON-WARNER, S., *Spinster,* Virago

BRITTON, J., *Language and Learning,* Pelican 1970

HOLLAND, N., *Five Readers Reading,* Yale University Press, 1975

SQUIRE, J., *The Responses of Adolescents While Reading Four Short Stories,* (Research Report No.2) N.C.T.E. 1964

STEEDMAN, C., *The Tidy House; Little Girls Writing,* Virago 1982

Sex-Differentiated Knowledge

ADAMS, C., LAURIKIETIS, R., *The Gender Trap: A Closer Look at Sex Roles;* Book 3, Messages and Images, Virago 1980

BELOTTI, E., *Little Girls,* Writers and Readers Co-op 1975

BYRNE, E., *Women and Education,* Tavistock Publications 1978

CANNAN, C., *Female from Birth,* TES 14.1.1972.

CHETWYND, J., *The Sex Role System,* Routledge and Kegan Paul 1978

CLARRICOATES, K., *Dinosaurs in the Classroom,* in Women's Studies International Quarterly 1978 Vol.1 pp. 353-364

DEEM, R., *Women and Schooling,* Routledge and Kegan Paul 1978

DEEM, R., *Schooling for Women's Work,* Routledge and Kegan Paul 1980

DELAMONT, S., *Sex Roles and the School,* Methuen 1980

HARNETT, O., *Sex Role Stereotyping,* Tavistock Publications, 1979

HODGEON, J., *A Woman's World?* A report on a Project in Cleveland Nurseries on Sex Differentiation in the Early Years 1984

I.L.E.A. *Gender and English: Resources for the English Department*

MACOBY, E., *The Development of Sex Differences,* Stamford University Press, 1969

MARGARET SANDRA, *Boys Underachievement in English:* MA Thesis. University of London, Institute of Education 1981

MARGARET SANDRA, *She's Good at English — Is English Good For Her?,* TLK19

MARLAND, M., (ed) *Sex Differentiation and Schooling,* Heinemann Educational 1983

MCROBBIE, A., *Working Class Girls and the Culture of Femininity* in Women Take Issue. Hutchinson University Press 1978

NICHOLSON, J., *What Society Does to Girls,* Virago, 1975

SHARPE, S., *Just Like a Girl,* Penguin 1976

SPARE RIB 131 June 1983 *Sexual Harassment in Schools.* This article has a very useful set of guidelines for action.

SPENDER, D., & ELIZABETH, S., (eds) *Learning to Lose: Sexism and Education,* The Women's Press, 1980

SPENDER, D., *Invisible Women: The Schooling Scandal,* Writers & Readers Co-op 1982

SPENDER, D., *Men's Studies Modified: The Impact of Feminism on the Academic Disciplines.* Pergamon Press 1982

STACEY, J., *And Jill Came Tumbling After: Sexism in American Education,* Dell, New York 1974

STANWORTH, M., *Gender and Schooling: A Study of Sexual Divisions in the Classroom,* WRRC 1981

WHYLD, J., (ed) *Sexism in the Secondary School Curriculum* Harper and Row 1983

WOLPE, A., *Some Processes in Sexist Education,* WRRC 1977

Language and Gender

COUSSINS, J., *What's In A Name*, NCCL
KAPLAN, C., *"Language and Gender"* in Papers on Patriarchy, Women's Publishing Collective 1976
LAKOFF, R., *Language and Woman's Place*, Harper and Row 1975
MILLER, C., & SWIFT, K., *Words and Women*, Penguin, 1979
MILLER, C., & SWIFT, K., *The Handbook of Non-Sexist Writing for Writers, Editors and Speakers*, The Women's Press, 1981
SPENDER, D., *Man Made Language*, Routledge and Kegan Paul, 1980
THORNE, B., *Language and Sex: Difference and Dominance*, Newbury House, Rowley Mass

Feminism and Sexual Politics

BEAUVOIR, S., *The Second Sex*, Penguin 1972
BOSTOCK, E., *Talking About Women*, Wayland 1973
BRISTOL Women's Studies Group, *Half the Sky: An Introduction to Women's Studies*, Virago 1979
DALY, M., *Gyn-Ecology: The Meta-Ethics of Radical Feminism*, The Women's Press 1979
FIRESTONE, S., *The Dialectic Of Sex*, The Women's Press 1979
FRIEDAN, B., *The Feminine Mystique*, Penguin, 1968
MILLETT, K., *Sexual Politics*, Virago, 1979
MITCHELL, J., *The Rights and Wrongs of Women*, Penguin, 1976
RICH, A., *Of Woman Born*, Virago, 1977
TURNBULL, A., *Women With A Past*, WRRC, 1981
WILSON, A., *Finding a Voice: Asian Women in Britain*, Virago, 1978

Women and Writing

BAMBARA, T. (ed) *Black Women: An Anthology*, Mentor New York, 1970
MOERS, Ellen,. *Literary Women*, The Women's Press, 1976
OLSEN, Tillie, *Silences*, Virago, 1980
SHOWALTER, Elaine, *A Literature of Their Own*, Virago, 1978
WOOLF, V., *Women and Writing* (ed. Michelle Barratt), The Women's Press, 1978

Equal Opportunities

CAMPBELL, B., *Are Equal Opportunities Enough?*, City Limits December 11th-17th, 1982
COUSSINS, J., *Taking Liberties: A Teaching Pack for Boys and Girls on Equal Rights*, Virago, 1979
EDMUNDS, J., *Rights, Responsibilities and the Law*, Nelson, 1982

Images of Women

BERGER, John, *Ways of Seeing*, Pelican, 1972
KING, J., *Is This Your Life? Images of Women in the Media*, Virago, 1977
KUHN, A., *Women's Pictures: Feminism and the Cinema*, RKP 1982

Feminist Research and Studies

ADAMS, C., & HARGREAVE, D., (COMPILERS) *Herstudies: a resources list for teachers of History and Social Sciences*, available from I.L.E.A. History and Social Science Teachers' Centre
FYSON, L., GREENHILL S. AND N., *Investigating Society: People Talking*, MacMillan, 1979
ROBERTS, H., (ed) *Doing Feminist Research*, Routledge and Kegan Paul, 1981

Pastoral Care

MARLAND, M., *Pastoral Care*, Heinemann Educational 1979
MORRIS, B., *The Caring Element in the Education System*, in Residential Establishments: the Evolving of Caring Systems ed. Hunter and Ainsworth.

The Contributors

Julia Hodgson has taught in infant and nursery schools for twelve years. She recently completed a project sponsored by the Equal Opportunities Commission and Cleveland County on sex differentiation in nursery units. She teaches at Sunnyside Primary School, Middlesborough.

Hilary Minns is Headteacher of Courthouse Green Primary School in Coventry and has taught in Primary Schools for sixteen years.

Linda Harland was born in 1947, brought up and educated in Nottingham, and has been involved with Special Needs and primary education in Hertfordshire, Haringey and Brent for the last eleven years. She is currently working for the Brent Learning Resources Service.

Bridget Baines was brought up in Zimbabwe and has taught English for ten years in comprehensive schools in the West Midlands. She is currently working at Exeter University School of Education on a curriculum research project, evaluating the Exeter Technical and Vocational Education Initiative.

Elaine Millard was born in 1945 and has been teaching English at Northern Comprehensive Schools since 1968. She is currently teaching at Bilborough Sixth form College, Nottingham.

Heather Morris has worked for Heinemann Educational Books for five years and is English and Drama editor.

Valerie Hey taught in Further and Secondary Education full-time between 1971-78. Between 1978-80 she taught part-time in Women's Studies for the W.E.A. In 1980 she moved to London and completed an M.A. in Women's Studies at the University of Kent at Canterbury in 1982. She is currently working for a Ph.D. on young women's cultural resistances and reponses to oppression.

Jan Sargeant was a sabbatical Vice-President of the city of Manchester College Students' Union 1977-78. She taught at a Birmingham Comprehensive School for three and a half years and is now teaching English at a school in Chesterfield, Derbyshire.

Margaret Sandra is an advisory English teacher and Labour Councillor in South London, born and bred in North London. She has taught in London Comprehensives since 1964, during which time she has been a member of the *Teaching London Kids* Collective and the London Association for the Teaching of English.

Pat Barrett is an English Adviser. She has taught in Primary and Secondary Schools and in a College of Education. At present, she is the Membership Secretary of N.A.T.E.

Cath Jackson is a free-lance illustrator, who lives and works in London.

National Association for the Teaching of English

WHAT DOES IT MEAN TO YOU?

Why not join NATE now and enjoy the full benefits of membership.
You gain:

1. A professional subject association to represent your views on every aspect of English teaching.

2. Three copies annually of English in Education and a full subscription to the English Magazine to keep you up to date with news, reviews, opinion and debate.

3. Three copies annually of the NATE Newsletter: an informal round-up of what's happening where amongst NATE branches, and who does what elsewhere, together with some cryptic labour-saving reviews of what's new in print.

4. Free NATE publications on matters of concern to all English teachers.

5. Local branch membership and a share in local activities if you so wish.

6. Attendance at the Annual Course and Conference at the reduced rate for NATE members.

Apply for membership now.

Simply write for an application form to:
NATE
49 Broomgrove Road
Sheffield S10 2NA